Privacy in the Computer Age

G L Simons

PUBLISHED BY NCC PUBLICATIONS

British Library Cataloguing in Publication Data

Simons, G.L.
Privacy in the computer age.
1. Privacy, Right of 2. Data base management
I. Title
323.44'83 JC597

ISBN 0-85012-348-8

First published in 1982 by:

NCC Publications, The National Computing Centre Limited, Oxford Road, Manchester M1 7ED, England.

Typeset in 11pt Times Roman by Printsave (Lancashire) Limited, 19A Whalley Road, Accrington, Lancashire and printed by UPS Blackburn Limited, 76-80 Northgate, Blackburn, Lancashire.

ISBN 0-85012-348-8

Acknowledgements

This book is largely based on material derived from journal articles, books and government publications. These are listed in the Bibliography (Appendix 1). I am grateful to Stuart Anderson of the Technical Authors Group (Scotland) for permission to use material from the TAG(S) Occasional Publication No. 1, 'The Police Use of Computers' (my Table 1 is an extract from that publication).

I am also particularly grateful to NCC staff for their help with this project. Tony Elbra (Privacy and Security Division) made his accumulated literature available for research, and Michael Wood (Manager, Privacy and Security Division) read the typescript in draft, making various useful comments. Thanks are also due to Michael Wood and Tony Elbra for permission to reproduce (as Appendix 2) the NCC comments on the Government White Paper (Cmnd 8539).

I discussed privacy auditing with Ian Douglas (Privacy and Security Division) and his comments were very useful. I am grateful for permission to draw extensively on the recent report, 'The External Auditor as Privacy Inspector' (Deloitte Haskins & Sells and NCC) for Appendix 3.

Again, thanks are due to Christine Marshall (Publications Division) for assisting with research and for checking the material at various stages; and to Janice Wooding (Publications Division) for drawing my attention to relevant material appearing in current journals.

Geoff Simons
Chief Editor
NCC Publications

Introduction

Protection of individual privacy is a complex issue, bearing as it does on technological developments, computer systems design, commerce, legislation and human rights. There is a growing recognition throughout the developed world of the need for effective legislation in this field, but there is much debate about the form this legislation should take. Existing legislation varies widely from one country to another. In general it is acknowledged that a balance must be struck between safeguarding the civil rights of individuals (and groups) in society and allowing the State to conduct, with minimum interference, its legitimate and necessary activities (such as tax administration and law enforcement).

This book aims to indicate the areas of concern, to chart the background to the current debate, and to outline current proposals for legislation. The main focus is on the UK scene, though the issues at stake have a universal relevance and some indication is given of the prevailing situation in other countries. As an introductory book, this publication can only sketch some of the privacy and data protection milestones on the route to the present situation. Readers interested in a more detailed treatment should refer to the cited source material.

It is hoped that this book will serve as a contribution to the current UK debate on privacy and data protection, not least in highlighting matters of concern to a wide range of public opinion. The UK Government has declared its intention to legislate in this field. It is obviously important that the forthcoming legislation achieve its declared aims as effectively and comprehensively as possible.

Contents

1 Background

GENERAL

Privacy is a human rights issue, relating as it does to the freedom of the individual in society. At one level it throws into focus an apparent conflict between the needs of the state and the needs of the citizen. Simply put, the state needs to monitor and control, whereas the citizen needs to be left alone. 'The state's interests are served by the need to know as much about us as possible, our own by reticence about ourselves' (Madgwick and Smythe, 1974).

It is obvious that freedom has to be constrained in various ways in the interest of the community: in most societies, the freedom to assault or to rob is discouraged both by public feeling and by law. Freedom of speech, often upheld, is usually constrained in one way or another, eg by considerations of defamation, sedition, blasphemy or racial incitement. Similarly, the human need to be left alone is typically constrained by the government need to collect information about people – for such purposes as tax administration and law enforcement. And particular organisations (such as hospitals, employer companies and credit agencies) need to collect information which, were it made freely available, could damage individual interests. Clearly, such aspects as confidentiality, the accuracy of collected information and the security of manual or computer systems in which information is held, are vitally relevant to the question of privacy. Government attitudes to these topics determine with what commitment legislative and other measures are introduced in this field.

The privacy question has been thrown into sharp relief by advances in computing. It is now possible to store vast amounts of information on computer file and to rapidly retrieve such information, or selected parts of it, for particular purposes. Networking can now link seemingly disparate computer systems, allowing a user of one system to access information on another. Increasingly, computers can 'talk to' each other, trading information, often across national boundaries. Computer developments are having a growing impact on society, not least on the relationship between the citizen and a wide range of social institutions, including government. The topic of privacy is particularly sensitive to this impact.

THE CONCEPT OF PRIVACY

The privacy of the individual has been a developing concept for many years. One early definition of privacy as 'the right to be let alone' was proposed by the American Judge Cooley (*Torts*, 1888). An expanded definition was presented in a California suit (Kerby v Hal Roach Studios, 1942) where privacy was seen as 'the right to live one's life in seclusion, without being subjected to unwarranted or undesired publicity. In short it is the right to be let alone'. Such generalised definitions are relatively unhelpful in relation to modern computer technology.

T L Yang (1966) proposed that 'invasion of privacy as a legal term is in reality nothing more than a canopy under which four distinct wrongs are gathered', and Professor Prosser (*Law of Torts*, 1955) has grouped the classification of these wrongs under four categories:

— the intrusion of an individual's physical solitude and seclusion . . . *whether or not by physical presence* (original italics);

— the violation of ordinary decencies by disclosure of an individual's personal and private facts . . .;

— acts which put an individual in a false light in the public eye, such as the unauthorised use of his name to support, for example, a public petition . . .;

— the appropriation of some element of the individual's personality (such as his name, likeness, voice or conduct) for the advantage of another.

Clearly some of these categories are more relevant than others to the development of computerised files of information. A somewhat different emphasis was presented by a 1967 panel on Privacy and Behavioural Research reporting to the US President's Office of Science and Technology: 'The right to privacy is the right of the individual to decide for himself how much he will share with others his thoughts, his feelings, and the facts of his personal life . . .'. This panel recognised that the nature of privacy varied, depending upon a wide range of social and other circumstances.

The first international conference to study the privacy question was held in Stockholm in 1967. This conference, organised by the International Commission of Jurists, was attended by legal experts from many countries. It was urged that the Right to Privacy should be held as one of the fundamental rights of mankind, and that all countries should 'take appropriate measures to protect by legislation or other means the right to privacy in all its different aspects and to prescribe the civil remedies and criminal sanctions required for its protection'. Here it was proposed that the individual should have the right to be protected against:

— interference with the individual's private, family or home life;

— interference with one's physical or mental integrity or one's moral or intellectual freedom;

— attacks on one's honour and reputation;

— being placed in a false light;

— the disclosure of irrelevant embarrassing facts relating to one's private life;

— spying, prying, watching and besetting;

— interference with correspondence;

— misuse of private correspondence, written or oral;

— disclosure of information given or received by the individual in circumstances of professional confidence.

These provisions should be interpreted as relating to such activities as search of the person, medical examinations, intercepting correspondence, telephone tapping, use of electronic surveillance devices, public disclosure of private facts, etc.

It should be evident that the concept of privacy is complex, meaning different things to different people. The concept predates computer technology but is highlighted by the potential of modern data processing systems. It bears on the relationships between citizens, and between citizens and social institutions (such as government, police, hospitals and banks). In particular it bears on the relationship between the citizen and authority, signalling the degree of freedom enjoyed by the individual in the modern state. Part of the significance of Orwell's *1984* lies in how the total deprivation of personal privacy is portrayed.

Modern societies have legitimate claims on information about individuals. Without appropriate information, it would be impossible to administer social services, to implement educational and health programmes, or to safeguard civic order and national security. But there are many ways in which abuse of personal privacy can occur. It is essential to define the legitimate claims of government and other bodies within a framework of appropriate legislative and institutional safeguards.

THE IMPACT OF COMPUTING

Increasing attention is being given to the social impact of computing. For example, Kling (1982) examines the 'roles of computer technologies in the workplace, in decision-making, in altering power relationships and in influencing personal privacy'. In this paper a range of empirical studies are reviewed. It is suggested that, during the 1960s, efforts to examine personal privacy and computing were largely speculative, but that a common set of beliefs about the influence of computer use on organisational record-keeping systems was discernible:

- organisations employing automated record-keeping systems would gather more personally-sensitive information about individuals;
- such organisations could more easily share with each other information about selected individuals;

— joint efforts of more organisations collecting increasing amounts of information and sharing it casually would lead to serious losses of individual privacy.

In the early-1970s, various studies of record-keeping in large computer-using organisations were published. For instance, Westin and Baker (1972) in the US studied fifty-five organisations, with key officials being invited to describe the record-keeping practices. Detailed accounts of fourteen organisations – including police agencies, a large bank, a state motor vehicle registry, an insurance firm and a credit-reporting firm – were reported. Another study (Rule, 1974) focused on police agencies, insurance firms, state motor vehicle agencies and credit companies.

At that time the studies suggested that technical feasibility plays only a small role in influencing the types of records collected and shared by computer-using organisations. It was further observed that major institutional barriers existed to prevent organisations from routinely pooling information about individuals. Westin and Baker concluded in this context that the public need not worry about erosion of privacy, providing that individuals could check information about them and providing that individuals could be involved in controlling the uses to which the information was put.* They recommended that procedural safeguards (in 'hygienically acceptable' systems) be provided, rather than restrictions be imposed on the types of record-keeping systems that should or should not be developed. (This type of recommendation is generally held to have influenced most subsequent US privacy legislation, such as the 1974 Federal Privacy Act.)

By contrast, Rule saw as a principal concern the development of automated systems for mass surveillance and social control in advanced countries, recognising that large bureaucratic organisations could be enlisted to aid such tasks (with formal record-keeping systems serving as a 'critical instrument'). And he notes, for instance, that credit-reporting firms are obliged to provide some derogatory information to aid credit grantors in their selection of the most credit-worthy individuals.

Rule proposes that the 'surveillance capacity' of an information system can be defined by the 'sheer amount of meaningful personal

* In due course it became clear that these were rather large provisos.

data available on those with whom the system must deal', 'the effective centralisation of data resources', 'the speed of information flow and decision-making within the system' and 'the points of contact between system and clientèle'. As organisations expand, they increasingly rely upon automated information systems.

There is also attention, in the Rule study (1974), to the institutionalised practices that make it difficult for the public to understand how information about them is handled. Privacy of organisational practices, as well as of individual records, can be represented as a key characteristic of modern organisations. And Rule has pointed out that many organisations, despite claiming that their information is confidential, readily make it available to certain people who may be able to use it. Hence, 'reports [of consumer credit reporting agencies] are available to any agency or individual who appears to be a grantor of credit. Likewise, information held . . . by the British police is . . . supplied routinely to many employers and professional bodies, as well as accidentally or unofficially to other users'.

Such concerns may be seen as ever more pressing in circumstances where increasing use is being made of complex computer systems to store information about individuals. A central purpose of computerised information systems is to speed the flow of information. It has long been recognised that this can occur in ways that interfere with the privacy of citizens.

By 1970 the characteristics of new computer systems were beginning to concern observers with an interest in privacy and security. It was clear that businesses and government departments were starting to implement more sensitive computer applications than ever before, aided by increasingly powerful memory devices. Terminals were being connected to computers in increasing numbers, and a growing range of users were able to share computer resources. At the same time, provisions for auditing computer systems seemed inadequate.

Today computers are continuing to increase in numbers and scope (well over a million computers in use in the US alone, with many systems capable of accessing millions of characters of information in a fraction of a microsecond). It is anticipated that by the end of the 1980s, more than 100 million computers will be operating in the US. Many of these systems will operate in distributed data networks which put processing power in the hands of those who need it – company chairmen, bank clerks, hospital administrators, policemen, etc. A late-1970s report suggested that the dollar value of shipments of distributed data processing products will grow at a compounded growth rate of 59 per cent per year. A number of observers have noted that privacy and security are more difficult to control in a distributed environment. For example, Lobel (1982) points out that:

— more critical information about business and personnel matters will be removed from the individual's physical control. Information will be held in a computer database somewhere in a network, rather than in a locked desk or cabinet;

— more people will have access to the computer, ie they will have potential access to sensitive information;

— the person intent on obtaining sensitive information has a good chance of remaining anonymous, not needing to be physically present on company or government property;

— information errors, present in all systems, will spread through a distributed network 'at electronic speed';

— as a distributed data processing system expands into more and more areas, people become more dependent upon it – so the risks increase.

The major factor in the growing interest in privacy in recent years is the rapid development of computer technology. In particular, the range and scope of record-keeping have been dramatically enlarged. Dangers to privacy in storing ever more information about individuals have been perceived, and a variety of safeguards – ranging from technical security measures to legislation – have been developed (see below).

AREAS OF CONCERN

The effective safeguarding of individual privacy in modern society can only be achieved by giving attention to a number of seemingly disparate areas. Some of these are considered in Chapter 2 but can be briefly indicated here.

The Police

The relationship between the forces of social control and private citizens is a nice index of the degree of freedom in a society – with the spectrum running from full democratic control over all police activity at one extreme to the totalitarian 'police state' at the other. It may be assumed that no country occupies either extreme, but that the mix of democratic control and repressive activity varies from one country to another and from time to time.

In this context we may ask:

What types of information do the police collect about private citizens?

What classes of people interest the police? Are these solely 'criminal elements' or do they also include political and social-protest factions (eg 'extremist' MPs, trade union leaders, CND protesters, gay activists, 'dissidents' of whatever hue)?

Do private citizens have the means to check whether they appear in police files? Do they have the means to check whether recorded information about them is accurate? And can they insist that it be corrected?

Are the police able to access files held by other institutions (eg hospitals)? This is potentially easy to accomplish using modern computer networking methods.

What uses do the police make of the information they collect? Are routine procedures established for particular types of information?

In general, what rules or principles govern the collection by the police of information about private citizens? What democratic or political control exists over police activity in these areas?

Police activity is necessarily wide-ranging – concerned, as it must be, with many different types of tasks (from apprehending petty robbers to arresting international terrorists). This suggests that police information-gathering is equally wide-ranging and that in many circumstances there can be a manifest political dimension. Concern has been expressed about the use by MI5 of modern computing facilities (see Chapter 2), just as observers have questioned police computing in other areas.

The courts, too, bear on the privacy issue. Information, often of a highly sensitive and personal nature, is gathered in preparation for a trial or court hearing. This information is invariably held on file. Who has access to it? For what purpose? What are the safeguards?

Medical Care

Effective hospital and other forms of medical care depend upon adequate information about patients. Again this information is often highly personal, and we may ask:

What types of personal information are collected by hospital staff, GPs and other medical practitioners? Is this information strictly relevant to the cases in question? Can patients inspect their records?

How is the information stored and who has access to it? How secure is the record-keeping system? Does it link in to a broader network? Could someone outside the hospital (or clinic or GP's surgery) have access to the stored information?

Does the hospital make information available to other organisations, such as the police or employers?

What are the rules that govern computerised files of information in hospitals and other health care organisations? Who draws up the rules? What are the system and institutional safeguards against abuse?

Concern has been expressed, not least by the BMA, that inadequate attention is being paid by government to the protection of medical information. Developments in computer technology have focused attention on privacy in this area.

Government Departments

Governments collect information to administer social services, taxation policies, educational schemes, employment programmes and the like.

In July 1982 it was reported that the Government was planning to computerise the entire social security system over the next decade.

The declared intention was to install a microcomputer in each benefit office to help to handle the range of more than thirty different types of benefits paid to more than 21 million people every week. One consequence of the intended computerisation will be to integrate existing child benefit and pensions claims, already on computers.

Six experimental 'claimants computers' are being installed by the Department of Health and Social Security to help people to obtain advice about benefits. The Witham constituents of Mr Tony Newton, a junior social security minister, will be among the first with access to one of these computers. Others are to be installed in Manchester, London and Scotland.

The Government intends to publish a strategy paper outlining the computerisation plans. The aim will be to improve service to claimants, to enhance job satisfaction for clerical staff, to make the DHSS more efficient and to save government money. Supplementary benefits claimants may be expected to gain, as the microcomputers should enable staff to process claims quickly. Part of the Department's S Manual on claimants' entitlements may also be put on a computer. The Government has emphasised that it does not intend to use the computers to investigate 'social security scroungers' or to give the investigators special computers to investigate claimants they suspect of fraud.

The Inland Revenue is another Government department where extensive computerisation is envisaged. The IR's plan to computerise the UK PAYE system is, in July 1982, in its second year of implementation. The basic plan, announced by the Government in November 1980, is for the IR to set up twelve regional computer centres. All of the 600 local tax offices in the country will be assigned by region to one of these centres. Staff in the local offices will then be connected to the central processors through desktop visual display units. It will be helpful to the IR to be able to move information around the system. Eventually, direct machine/machine communication will take place within the regional centres and between the centres and a central node or routeing centre.

As part of the implementation plan, three ICL 2966 computers have already been delivered to Telford, Shropshire, where the IR has a purpose-built centre for systems testing and applications development. The intention is for the IR to take forty-seven machines by late 1985. It has been emphasised that the proposed nationwide implementation does not mean that any tax inspector will have total access to all the data on all the PAYE taxpayers in the country (Steve Matheson, overseeing the project, has commented: 'This anxiety, which I hear expressed over and over, has no basis. Not only would the sheer numbers of taxpayers in the country make nonsense of this, but the tax inspectors in each office will still be subject to the same checks and restrictions they are under at present').

Again the same questions can be asked – What information is collected? How is it stored? Who has access to it? For what purposes? And what are the safeguards?

Personnel Departments

The personnel departments of companies and other employers collect considerable amounts of information about individuals. Often this information is highly sensitive: it can, for instance, include medical histories (employees are sometimes asked to give permission to company medical staff to contact the employees' GPs to obtain medical information). Again it can be asked whether all the information collected by employers is strictly relevant to their purposes? And how is the information stored? Can employees inspect information held on them? Who has access to it? Do employers make sensitive information available to other employers – in, for example, helping managements to decide whom to hire and fire? In all cases, what are the safeguards?

Banks

Banks and other financial institutions necessarily gain much insight into personal lifestyles. It is often an easy matter for banks to know a person's expenditure on alcoholic drink, holidays, cars, restaurants, etc. Is the person servicing debts, paying alimony, paying fines to a court, etc? In many cases the bank will know. For example, how does a bank store information on standing orders, agreed overdraft arrangements and such like? Do other branches have access to such information? Do institutions investigating credit worthiness? Do the police? Can nominal limitations on access be circumvented? By bank employees? By people outside the organisation? What are the policies on rules and safeguards? Some of the questions are general and some bear specifically on the nature of banking institutions.

Other Organisations

Wherever people interact with organisations or institutions in society there is an inevitable exchange of information. If a person subscribes to a book club, a magazine, a protest organisation, an academic association, etc, then information will be held about the person. A newsagent may feel able to say something about the sexual or political tastes of regular clients and subscribers to newspapers. How does he record information about, for example, subscriptions to controversial newspapers? Who has access to the information? How readily would the information be divulged to outside interests, such as potential employers, social security investigators and the police?

It is clear that the privacy question has many facets, and that to a large extent this has impeded legislation and other effective safeguards. At the same time it is reasonable to expect governments to be interested in developing effective protection for an important and widely recognised human right. It may be inappropriate to expect legislation to cover the local newsagent or the local tennis club, but whenever sensitive personal information is stored – today increasingly in computer-based systems – it is reasonable to expect governments to be interested in introducing and upholding suitable data protection measures.

SAFEGUARDS

Awareness of the possible (or actual) abuse of computer systems has stimulated the development of a wide range of safeguards. The privacy of the individual – one example of a human right that may be under threat – can be protected in various ways.

Technical

A principal approach is to design *secure** systems, ie systems that

* Security is a key area of NCC interest. In recent years the Centre has published nearly twenty books on various aspects of security (see the NCC book catalogue).

can prevent illicit (or illegal) access to information. Moves towards distributed processing are encouraging systems designers to develop hardware and software that are 'responsible' and 'secure'. Recent research has focused on the design of secure communications networks, secure front-end network processors, and the technology of certifiably secure systems. There is pressure on suppliers to ensure that security will be a key feature of systems to be launched in the future. Often security features are involved in a trade-off situation: for example, cost and performance can be traded off for more security if this is held to be necessary. At the same time it is often suggested that no system can be 100 per cent secure.

Various techniques can be used to protect sensitive information held in computer files. For example, emphasis has been given to the importance of encryption in this area (Pritchard, 1980). With data encryption, data is converted from its original form (termed 'plain text' or 'clear text') into what is intended to be a secret form (termed 'cipher text'). The encryption process uses an algorithm (to convert the text) and a key (eg a string of characters). Other techniques rely upon building a range of security routines into operating systems, though anxiety has been expressed that such routines are not always as secure as they might be.

One American scare (reported by John Lamb, 1982; and other observers) involved the Unix operating system and a particular type of terminal. Students at the University of California devised a way of impersonating system users without knowing their passwords, and so of gaining access to 'protected' computer files. The security problem that this incident illustrated is thought to be one of hundreds. Security consultant Ian Douglas (of NCC) has noted: 'There have been a number of cases where operating systems have been broken, especially in universities. Many of these computer studies students have become fed up with computers and are now training as managers or accountants. The auditing profession is very concerned'.

Legislative

Potential computer criminals can be discouraged by systems incorporating a range of security features – and they can also be discouraged by legislation (see Chapters 4 and 5). In 1979, President Carter announced 'sweeping proposals to protect the privacy of individuals'. In following the example of several other countries (notably Sweden), he recognised that the challenge is 'to provide privacy safeguards that respond to . . . social changes without disrupting the essential flow of information'. It should be emphasised that the problem of computer abuse cannot be solved solely by technical measures; the question of human motivation is highly relevant – which suggests a place for effective legislative control in this area.

Sweden adopted a Data Act in 1973, which requires, amongst other things, that all personal information files be licensed. The approval procedures, assigned to a special Data Inspection Board, include specification of use of the data and clear directives governing conditions of use, access and maintenance. In recent years, legislation in other Western European countries has been moving in a similar direction.

SUMMARY

The privacy of the individual is an important human right. It has always been under threat in various ways but today these dangers are given added scope by the power of modern data processing systems. Personal privacy can be threatened by virtue of the detailed information held in computerised files by such institutions as government, hospitals, banks and the police. A number of different types of safeguards exist and are being constantly developed. Some of these relate specifically to hardware and software features, whereas others relate to codes of conduct or legislation.

2 Some Areas of Concern

GENERAL

In modern society there are many ways in which the privacy of the individual can be threatened. Developments in technology have made it easier to 'bug' a person's home or office, to listen in to telephone or other conversations, and to record masses of personal information for easy access. Computer technology in particular has made it possible for both private and public organisations to collect – for many different purposes – vast amounts of information about people.

The interaction of the citizen with social organisations – schools, colleges, banks, credit companies, government departments, clubs, hospitals, the police, etc – requires that the citizen be willing to make information available. Much of this information is trivial, but some of it is sensitive and important. The unwarranted disclosure of *some* types of personal information may affect a person's employment prospects, marriage, treatment in the courts, credit rating, and public reputation. It is clear that when a person provides information to an organisation, the person has an interest in the security of that information, and in knowing to whom the information is available. And it is also necessary to know that the information has been recorded accurately, that the upright pillar of society is not confused with an international terrorist of the same name.

The citizen may also be concerned that personal information might be held in unsuspected data banks. Information may be supplied for one computer file and finish up in another.

Increasingly, modern data processing systems can 'talk to' each other: sometimes ingenious programmers can cause computer systems to communicate in ways, and to an extent, not originally envisaged by the system designers.

In summary, the citizen needs to know:

— what information about that citizen is held;

— why that information is held;

— where the information is held;

— who has access to the information (eg how secure is it? does the computer system connect to other systems – in the same organisation, elsewhere in the country, or across national boundaries?);

— what are the provisions for reviewing the system safeguards in the light of technological change;

— who is responsible in the organisation for ensuring the adequacy of the safeguards;

— what codes or laws exist to protect the information held in the organisations in question.

These legitimate concerns of the citizen can relate to the activities of a wide range of social bodies, company departments, commercial institutions, government offices, etc. This chapter highlights some social areas which have caused concern. It is not intended to provide an exhaustive discussion of all the social sectors that bear on the privacy question, but to indicate some of the key concerns that have focused attention on the need for government and other action in this area.

POLICE, MI5

General

The forces of law and order, by their very nature, touch on civil liberties in various ways. Society invests great powers in the police and the security forces: without adequate safeguards it is almost inevitable that such powers will be used, to a greater or lesser extent, in an excessively authoritarian or repressive fashion.

Privacy is only one aspect of civil liberties that bears on the relationship of the police to private citizens. And not all privacy matters, as we have seen, relate to the development and use of computer-based systems.

Use of Computers

The police in the UK (and elsewhere), in common with all other large-scale organisations in society, are increasingly resorting to computers for a variety of purposes. One example is how the *Police National Computer* (PNC) at Hendon is used for vehicle checks. Access to the PNC for a vehicle check provides the name and address of the registered owner and also a physical description of the vehicle. With this information the police can access the PNC for wanted or missing persons information and to check whether the vehicle is 'of interest' to the police (it may, for instance, have been stolen or involved in a crime). It is estimated that in 1982 there will be approximately 20 million vehicle checks and four million name checks made on the PNC. It is worth looking at the Police National Computer in detail*.

The latest PNC was installed at the Police National Computer Centre at Hendon in 1975. This system provides vehicle and criminal information to all the fifty-one constabularies in the UK via a network of 800 computer terminals sited in the various force headquarters. Some of the larger forces are using PNC terminals in the divisional stations. Most of the terminals are concentrated in the London area.

It is recognised that the PNC has been very successful as a source of basic information of various types. Development of local police computers has been aimed at achieving easier access to the PNC or at filling gaps in the PNC-supplied information. The stored information is organised into various indexes which can be accessed by feeding to the computer a partial description of the information required. A police officer typically supplies the number of a suspect car via radio to the force headquarters (in, say, Edinburgh or Manchester), whereupon another officer uses a terminal to transmit the number to the PNC. Information is quickly

* Much of what follows derives from the Pounder and Anderson TAG Report, 'The Police Use of Computers' (see Bibliography).

returned on the owner and car. This type of simple check is the most common use of the PNC, but a range of other checks can be carried out. (One facility provided by the PNC is a secure communication system between the various forces – the so-called 'message switch'.)

The PNC indexes are organised to provide various types of information. The most commonly used indexes include:

— *Stolen/suspect vehicles.* There are about 200,000 entries on this index, with information usually retrieved by feeding in the registration number. About seventy-five per cent of the entries do not relate to stolen vehicles, but to vehicles 'of interest' to the police. Information about vehicles can be entered in this index for eleven types of reason:

  — lost/stolen;
  — obtained by deception;
  — found vehicle;
  — vehicle repossessed by finance company;
  — suspected of being involved in a crime;
  — of interest to the police for a specific reason;
  — removed to the police pound;
  — street-to-street (removed by the police to another place);
  — vehicle used by the police;
  — blocked (information withheld);
  — seen vehicle (alternative to suspect vehicle and vehicle of particular interest).

A number of these categories are used by Special Branch, the small section of the police interested in the political activities of citizens. It is clear that enlargement of the scope of the PNC can enhance the monitoring capabilities of Special Branch. Pounder (1982) has suggested that most checks are made on moving vehicles: for example, in 1979 the Bedford Police performed 127,933 'stolen vehicle' checks but reported only 3710 stolen vehicles. One interpretation is that the index is used to provide intelligence rather than mainly to find stolen cars;

— *Stolen (chassis/engine) serial numbers.* This index carries much the same information as the stolen/suspect index, but access is via the chassis and engine numbers;

— *Vehicle owners.* This is a duplicate of the index held by the Driving and Vehicle Licensing Centre at Swansea. It carries about 20 million entries, and includes descriptive information on all vehicles registered in the UK and the name and address of the owner;

— *Fingerprints.* This index carries all criminal fingerprints held in the UK and is accessible via standard descriptions of fingerprints. This facility, only available to New Scotland Yard, returns a list of all potentially matching prints, once a description of a print in question has been provided. (New Scotland Yard has recently placed a £1.5 million contract with Logica to provide a system that will handle the Yard's collection of around 100,000 prints. The aim is to have the system – using the Focus fingerprint matching software – operational by the end of 1983. Logica is to supply the Metropolitan Police's fingerprint branch with twin Prime 750 minicomputers, four floating-point array processors, video equipment, etc. Logica is currently developing the vital comparison algorithms as well as simplifying the man/machine interface. Once installed, the system will allow a user to scan a disk file of fingerprints of known criminals and compare them with prints (or print fragments) found at the scene of a crime. The system finally prints out the names of the people whose prints show the best comparison. A final comparison is made with entries in the manual file, only a manual comparison currently being acceptable as valid evidence by the courts.);

— *Criminal names.* This index includes about four million names of criminals and their aliases. The stored information comprises a physical description for identification purposes (eg colour of skin, distinguishing marks, sex, height, etc), and a reference number for the full national Criminal Record Office paper file on the person;

— *Wanted/missing persons.* This index provides details of persons whom the police want to interview. A person may be included on this index for twelve types of reason:
  — wanted;
  — suspected;
  — failure to appear;
  — in custody;
  — desire to locate;
  — non-payment of fine;
  — life sentence out on licence;
  — missing from home;
  — absconder from institution;
  — armed forces deserter;
  — wanted on recall order to institution;
  — person refusing to disclose true identity.

  A number of 'warning indicators' also appear on this index.

Other indexes exist on the PNC and there are on-going plans for system enhancement. In 1977 the system's storage capacity was raised from four thousand million alphabetic characters to eight thousand million to accommodate new indexes. Accesses to the PNC dramatically increased that year because of the new storage capacity.

It is recognised that there is steady growth in the national computerisation of police intelligence records. One objective is to put local intelligence information on computers and to link these systems to the PNC. The present Home Secretary has declared himself in favour of the computerisation of intelligence data, though he has discouraged the linking of criminal records and criminal intelligence pending the outcome of the present privacy debate and the promised legislation. It has been suggested that the Police Scientific Development Branch of the Home Office is 'supervising the development of local computer systems with a built-in capacity to include intelligence records when the political climate is right' (Pallister, 1982).

In addition to the PNC facilities, the UK police forces make use of various *command and control computers*. More than two dozen such systems were operational by 1980, following a decade of research (an experimental system was installed in Birmingham in 1972, with later systems installed in Glasgow, Staffordshire and elsewhere). A typical command and control system is expected to have such facilities as:

— *Computer-aided dispatch.* In the West Midlands, for example, all emergency calls and other incidents are routed through consoles in a control room. Details are logged concerning the type of incident, the complainant, the location, etc. A *street index* is used to ascertain which subdivision should deal with the incident, a report being sent to the subdivision via the message switch (see below);

— *Message switch.* The command and control computers greatly enhance police communication capability. In the West Midlands system, the message switch, the PNC interface and the radio system together widen police access to the Police National Computer. The message switch facility allows any terminal on the West Midlands computer to communicate with the 54 terminals in the subdivisions and allows the terminals to access the PNC.

Operational command and control computers may be expected to improve police efficiency. It is clear that enhanced access to the PNC and the use of automatic street indexes coupled to an index of addresses 'of interest' extend the surveillance capabilities of the police. This has obvious relevance to privacy protection and other civil rights issues.

The growth in national police computing – in part stimulated by the Police Scientific Research Branch – still leaves local forces free to implement systems according to their judgement about local needs. The Police Committee of the Greater Manchester Police, for instance, selected Logica to supply a computerised criminal record system (MANCRO – Manchester Criminal Records Office), message switching system and PNC interface. The specification of the £3 million system was provided by Pactel. Five major applications are defined:

— MANCRO;

— information support;

— message handling;

— command and control;

— management reporting.

The specification written by the Pactel consultants envisages a criminal intelligence information system, to be based initially on a mixed computer/paper system but to move to the objective of a fully operational computer intelligence system. The system is intended to rely on six computers connected together in three pairs: if one computer in a pair fails, the other one takes over.

The first priority application, MANCRO, will be used via three indexes. The *nominal index*, accessed by providing a name, will be 'constructed from its inception so as to provide pointers to non computerised information'. Two other indexes – *Descriptive* (physical details) and *Modus Operandi* (method of working) – will be cross-linked to the nominal index to provide 'the full information held on each person'. Hence the system will be cross-referenced to the intelligence held by the divisional collator and will have links to other computer systems as they join the national computer network. As with other systems (eg the Lothian and Borders system), the Manchester facility will not initially hold criminal intelligence in the computer but will store details of where such information can be found in the paper files.

The fourth edition of *Police Use of Computers* (produced in 1979 by the Association of Chief Police Officers) lists seventeen (currently operational or planned) police computer systems listed under the Criminal Intelligence section. (The third edition defines criminal intelligence as 'all systems containing details of persons of interest to the police, but the subjects will not necessarily be convicted persons'.) Thus a distinction is made between criminal intelligence and criminal records. Table 1 (source: TAGS report — see Bibliography) provides some indication of existing police computers. The gaps in the table indicate 'the secrecy surrounding police computing in general'.

Force	Type	Date	Equipment	Comments
Avon+ Somerset	Admin		Mini computer Computer M/c Co	Access by 4 VDU's 50 million characters capacity
Bedford	C&C	1978	Dual Honeywell level 6	C&C Event; PNC link
Cambridge	Comms			PNC terminal concentrator; Full PNC link (1983)
Central Scotland	C&C	1973	Digital LSI 3/05	C&C — Unit Coded tone generator vehicle location
Cheshire	C&C	1981		During the '70s ran stolen property and criminal info on local authority machine
Cleveland	C&C	1978	Digital?	C&C – Event
	C&C	1981	Dual Data General Eclipse S140	PNC Link; Street index; free text; Claims to integrate Police communications
Derbyshire	C&C	Tender		May be stopped by local authority
Dorset	C&C	1977	Dual pdp 11/35	C&C – Event; Street Index; Message Switch
Durham	C&C	1980	GEC – Elliot	C&C – Event; PNC Link; Message Switch; Having problems getting the system to work
Essex	C&C	1978	Cyfas Ltd	20 terminals C&C – Event
	Admin	1981	Univac leased 80/3	Crime + accident stats; Personnel

Table 1 Survey of Police Computers (continued over)

Force	Type	Date	Equipment	Comments
Fife	C&C	1972	Cyfas Ltd	C&C – Unit Map display
Hampshire	C&C	1975	Digital	C&C – Unit
	CAP		Council m/c used	Hold criminal records indexed by M.O.
Humberside	C&C	1975	Computer Automation LSI 2/20	C&C – Unit
Kent	C&C	1977	Digital	C&C – Unit
Humberside and Kent	C&C	Tender		These two forces will buy identical machines
Lancashire	Admin		Use Council m/c	Probably personnel
	Local	1978	Mohawk Data	Skelmersdale project
	CAP	Tender		
Lothian and Borders	CAP	1981	Honeywell two DPS 8/20	PNC link, free text retrieval for crime information
Leicestershire	C&C	1978	Cyfas, CAI Alpha LSI-2	C&C – Unit
Lincolnshire	C&C, CAP	1978	ICL 2904	C&C – Unit; Nominal and M.O. Criminal Records Indexes; Can use L/A computer as a fall back
Manchester	CAP	1982	Logica Tandem	Large scale computer aided policing project
Merseyside	C&C	1981	Burroughs Mainframes Software Sciences Ltd	Street index by 1982. Access via 66 terminals
	CAP	1984		On the same machine but including criminal information

Table 1 Survey of Police Computers (continued over)

Force	Type	Date	Equipment	Comments
Metropolitan Police	C&C	1982	Univac 1100/62	Access via 600 terminals; 6 control rooms in New Scotland Yard and 70 control rooms in the Divisions.
	CAP	1980	CTL	'C' Division Machine
Northampton	C&C	1977	Data General	C&C – Unit
North Yorks	C&C		8503 Nova 3/12	PNC Interface
North-umberland	C&C	1980	SPL/Tandem	PNC Interface; Street index
Notts	C&C	1978		C&C – Unit; Propose extension to Event based
South Yorks	C&C			£800,000 C&C – Event
South Wales	C&C	1982	Dual Honeywell Level 6	C&C – Event; PNC link; 72 VDU's 34 printers in 3 control rooms and 27 stations
Staffordshire	C&C	1979	Dual Ferranti Argus	C&C – Event; PNC link; Criminal index to 'complement' PNC information; first county machine 8 VDU's in control room 18 in sub-divisions
Strathclyde	C&C	1978	Dual Ferranti Argus 700	C&C – Event; PNC Link; Initially only part of Glasgow, 1975 – all of Glasgow, 1978 all of force area
Suffolk	CAP	1977	GEC 4080	First experiment in computer aided policing; 16 VDU's 22 teleprinters; 736,000 messages in 1979/80. Free text on major incidents

Table 1 Survey of Police Computers (continued over)

Force	Type	Date	Equipment	Comments
Surrey	C&C	1979	CAI Alpha LSI-2	C&C – Unit
Sussex	C&C, CAP	1982	IAL, IBM Digital	PNC interface; street index criminal records. Proposal to use STAIRS (IBM free text system) for collators files and Criminal Intelligence
Tayside	CAP		ICL 1902t	Scottish Criminal Record Office pilot scheme. Criminal Intelligence
Thames Valley	CAP	1977	Honeywell	The 'collator' project
Ulster	C&C			Access via 240 terminals; information retrieval
Warwickshire	C&C	1976	Digital	C&C – Unit; Proposal to develop Event
West Mercia	CAP	1978	Data General Nova, upgrade to dual processor	C&C functions plus free text, criminal records and PNC interface
W Midlands	C&C	1977	Dual Ferranti Argus 700	Street index; PNC interface
	C&C	1978		Full C&C introduced access via 54 VDU's, 23 control desks at force HQ have access to mobiles via 8 VHF and 54 UHF channels
West Yorks	C&C		Dual Ferranti Argus	Information retrieval PNC interface
	Comms	1980	Format Communications MRS 100-16 and Texas 999/10	Links 40 stations at the moment, but is extensible to 256 stations

Table 1 Survey of Police Computers (continued)

MI5

In March 1982, details emerged about a secret MI5 computer capable of holding intelligence files on millions of people. The existence of this system was seen to pose 'grave questions about parliamentary democracy as well as personal data protection and privacy' (Connor, 11/3/82). A decade ago it was obvious that both MI5 (concerned with internal national security) and MI6 (external) were expanding the scope and number of their individual records. As far back as 1974 it was suggested that there could be no assurance that such records were 'either relevant or accurate' (Madgwick and Smythe, 1974) and that their main purpose seemed to be 'to keep tabs on politically suspect persons'. It is obvious that the secret accumulation of massive amounts of personal information, in circumstances where the individual has no means of checking the accuracy of the information, is highly relevant to the privacy question. The secret character of MI5 activity makes it virtually impossible – through, for example, parliamentary questioning – even to define the dimensions of the problem. A quotation from a one-time Home Secretary, Mr Henry Brooke – dating back nearly two decades – describes a situation that still largely prevails today:

> 'The Security Service is, after all, a secret service. That is part of its essence. Its cost is borne on the secret vote and one must bear in mind therefore that the number of parliamentary questions which could be put to me *with any hope of an answer being properly given* is very limited' (my italics).

The March 1982 revelations were of interest because, by the nature of the case, Parliament had at no time been informed of MI5's plans to install computers with 20,000 million bytes of on-line store. The ICL dual 2980s which constitute the system were acquired in secret. (Connor: 'No record of the 2980s exists on the confidential ICL files on the location of 2980 series computers in the UK'.) During the period of Sir Norman Lindop's deliberations on data protection (see Chaper 3), government departments were working to set up a massive and secret computer system. Negotiations for the ICL 2980s were completed by 1978.

Observers have speculated on why MI5 needs twenty gigabytes of on-line storage: the Ministry of Defence has only commented that the computers are used 'in the intelligence field'. One suggestion is that the MI5 system may be intended to have direct access to other central government computers, including those at the Department of Health and Social Security, the Inland Revenue, and the Department of Employment. Use of national insurance numbers as personal identifiers would expedite the transfer of personal information from one government computer system to another.

In 1975, a White Paper ('Computers: Safeguards for Privacy') denied that there were any plans to link computers together. At the same time it declared that 'exceptions' were 'computer systems kept for the strict purposes of national security: these are not described here'. Such exceptions would clearly include systems operated by MI5.

Questions in Parliament, protests by MPs (eg Skinner, Cryer, Meacher) and other efforts to throw light on government attitudes have not been fruitful. Prime Minister Margaret Thatcher has already indicated that she intends to say nothing whatever about MI5 activities.

Potential for Abuse

The necessary collection and storage of personal information by the police, MI5 and other law-and-order bodies has been greatly assisted by developments in computer technology. There are now in excess of 36 million entries on the Police National Computer, with around 220 government functions that involve the use of computerised personal information – each government data base is reckoned to contain between 10,000 and one million names. It has been claimed that by the end of the 1980s, about one fifth of London's population would be on computers operated by Scotland Yard. Michael Meacher, interested in 'firming up' Home Office ideas on data protection, has argued that legislative controls are needed to prevent any government, present or future, from abusing new technology – 'computerised data bases are vulnerable to espionage, eavesdropping and error'.

Information can be collected unlawfully, and lawfully-collected information can be inaccurate – through error or because a person's circumstances may change. Such possibilities may cause an individual to lose a job, to be denied promotion, to be refused a credit card, etc – through erroneous information of which he is unaware.

Systems may contain erroneous details about individuals simply because of human error. And information may be wrong, or tampered with, because of deliberate abuse. Pounder and Anderson (1982) have drawn attention to documented cases of abuse, involving the Police National Computer, by ex-police officers. In one case (reported in *New Statesman*, 23/10/81) ex-officers of the Thames Valley force allowed vehicles to be checked, using the PNC, as part of a private investigation. Chief Inspector P A Fraser of Merseyside Police (in *The Behavioural Implications of Computers*, Home Office Library) has highlighted other cases showing how abuse of computer systems can occur and how such abuse can be covered up.

One such abuse relates to a system in which officers were allowed fairly free access to the system and were permitted to add entries. A number of false entries were discovered: according to one entry, a senior police officer was to be taken to the nearest institute for the mentally insane if found wandering in the street – 'other such cases involved both real and fictitious characters'. But to avoid creating opposition to the newly implemented computer system 'no effort was made to identify the culprits'.

In another instance, also cited by Fraser, a local authority computer operator in West Germany accepted money to erase criminal convictions from the police system run on the local authority system. The arrangement was stopped when a policeman posed as a customer. However, the culprit was merely dismissed from his employment 'to avoid the embarrassment to the police that would have been caused by a court case'.

Scotland Yard, in late-1981, moved to change the procedure used by police to access the Police National Computer. Following a disclosure that members of the public were able to infiltrate the system, it was decided that police in London would have to make all requests for information by teleprinter. A report in the *Observer* claimed that highly confidential information was available to anyone knowing 'three childishly simple methods'. Three occasions were reported where a civilian posing as a detective sergeant obtained information over the telephone from Scotland Yard,

Brighton police and a Northumbria police station, and a spokesman for Scotland Yard agreed that information on a car registration number could have been given to an outsider ('the computer bureau number is well known to all police officers and our 20,000 civilian staff. We can only hope there have not been many abuses of it').

In October 1981 it was reported that a police officer in the Thames Valley force had been suspended following allegations that personal details on cars and criminal records had been leaked from police computers. The allegations were included in a dossier drawn up by Mr Julian Jacotter, a Labour member on the Thames Valley police authority. It was claimed that information from police computers could be sold for between £4 and £15 a check, but the Thames Valley police declared that access to its computers was restricted to a small number of serving officers (*Guardian*, 24/10/81). By April 1982 the enquiry was complete and a Thames Valley policeman faced disciplinary action on charges of leaking information and disobeying orders. Mr Jacotter emphasised the need for more adequate safeguards on police computers.

Early in 1982 the Home Secretary, William Whitelaw, was asked to investigate claims that the Police National Computer was being used illicitly to vet hotel and catering staff in London. The Hotel and Catering Workers Union had made representations to the Hamilton Labour MP, George Robertson ('I want to know in more specific terms whether there is a tight enough procedure to ensure that unauthorised people do not get access to the information in this computer').

It has often been suggested that files held by Special Branch are not totally secure. In 1982 more than one million Special Branch files were being transferred into a computer. In January 1982 the *Observer* reported that it had obtained details of a Special Branch file on a law-abiding member of the Social Democratic Party (10 years ago this person had helped to arrange anti-apartheid campaigns, but he has no criminal record). (Earlier it had been reported that local Special Branch files on anti-apartheid activists were compiled as standard police procedure in Devon and Cornwall, a practice that led to action by senior officers in the area.) After the *Observer* had informed Scotland Yard of the information it had received about the SDP member, the Special Branch suspended telephone enquiries, changed the number of its computer bureau, and ordered all enquiries to be made by teleprinter.

There have been a few cases in the past where Special Branch files have been obtained by employers. One instance was revealed in 1980 when the police apologised after an erroneous Special Branch file cost a woman a job with Taylor Woodrow, the construction firm. Such instances have highlighted the need for adequate control over how the police collect and store information. On occasions, as we have seen, such considerations have led to independent police initiatives in the interest of civil liberties.

In 1982 police in Devon and Cornwall began 'weeding out' files collated by the local Special Branch after senior officers decided that significant quantities of unnecessary information were held about law-abiding citizens. Several hundred files had accumulated over the last 15 to 20 years with only a small number relevant to police purposes (a senior police officer: 'I would guess about twenty'). The files included details on anti-nuclear activists, opponents of blood sports, and anti-apartheid activists. Evidence from Australia suggested that up to 80 per cent of Special Branch dossiers may be either improper, unnecessary or irrelevant.

It may be assumed that the 'weeding out' action by the Devon and Cornwall police, stimulated by the 'community policing' policies of the erstwhile Chief Constable, John Alderson, is not typical throughout the UK. The Metropolitan Special Branch, for instance, has secretly amassed 'political' files on a large scale and there is no suggestion that these are likely to be abandoned. Mr Merlyn Rees, the last Labour Home Secretary, said in the Commons (1978): 'The Special Branch collects information on those whom I think cause problems for the State'. This does not mean of course, that such people are acting illegally, or that the compiled information is always accurate. There are no UK laws to govern what political information the various Special Branches should secretly collect.

A judicial enquiry into Special Branch records compiled by police in South Australia was carried out in 1977 under the direction of a former Yorkshire Chief Constable, Mr Harold

Salisbury. The then Premier, Mr Don Dunstan, subsequently ordered destruction of most of the files when it was discovered that they covered all Labour politicians, half the supreme court judges, all 'left' or 'radical' university people, all prominent demonstrators, homosexuals, feminists, and divorce-law reformers.

It is obvious that certain types of information, even when accurately collected and recorded, can be damaging to the ordinary law-abiding citizen: examples can be given from various countries. Thomas Spohr, for instance, became one of 2.5 million West Germans in public employment to be screened by Nadis – the computer of the German security service – to ascertain whether they were 'hostile' to the constitution. He was dismissed from employment because he had urged people to vote for the legal West German Communist Party, had drawn a cartoon for a communist newspaper, and had come to Scotland to obtain support for his disciplinary court hearing. Half a million West Germans were called to such hearings to account for their actions – following the build-up of dossiers on computer-based and other systems.

The scope for abuse of police computer systems is wide-ranging, and it continues to grow with the development of computer technology in such areas as rapid access, enhanced storage and networking. Abuse can occur from within a police organisation and from without, and malice may or may not be present. Whatever the security safeguards, errors can occur in the collection and storing of information. Sometimes, for example, 'intelligence' may be based on rumour and hearsay, without adequate basis in fact. And where procedures, by their nature, are intended to be secret, the private citizen may be damaged by inaccurate or irrelevant information collected and stored without that person's knowledge.

HEALTH CARE

Medical information is often necessarily of a highly personal and sensitive nature. If illicitly divulged, it may affect a person's employment prospects, career progression, marriage, public reputation, etc. It may also affect a person's chances of conviction in court: it would be natural for the police to be interested in local hospital activity following a violent political demonstration. In the field of health care, as elsewhere, there is a need for adequate data protection.

The collection of medical information about citizens begins at birth. Much of this information is currently held in computerised systems – though, because of the sometimes controversial character of policy in this area, progress has been patchy.

The various Area Health Authorities (AHAs) are currently being encouraged to adopt a standard procedure when collecting information after a birth. Officially, the AHAs ceased to exist in April 1982, their activities being transferred to the District Health Authorities (DHAs) as part of a wide reorganisation of the National Health Service. In the past the AHAs collected the information required by the Department of Health and Social Security (DHSS), and have also collected other types of information. The DHAs are currently being recommended to use a standard Notification of Birth document, to be filled in by a midwife or doctor after a delivery. It is intended that the form should include four classes of personal information which are not required by the DHSS:

— whether the mother has had previous abortions;

— whether the child is born into a one-parent family;

— whether there are 'special factors' (such as the mental health of the mother);

— the ethnic group.

The AHAs have shown great disparities, from one region to another, in the amount of information they have collected. West Sussex, for example, has tended to collect only the DHSS essentials, whereas Nottingham records previous abortions, 'country of origin', legitimacy, and the occupations of the mother and father. There is a discernible trend towards recording a body of personal information that does not have obvious medical relevance. The fact that the AHAs without exception are currently using, or planning to use, computers to store an ever-growing quantity of personal information has clear relevance to data protection considerations.

The British Medical Association (BMA) has expressed concern about these developments and its Central Ethical Committee has put pressure on the Child Health Computing Committee, the organisation responsible for advising on computerisation matters.

A consequence has been that this working party has outlined three principles to be adopted:

- information should be held for the specific purpose of the continuing care of the patient, and should not be used for any other purpose without appropriate authorisation of the patient, parent or guardian;
- access to information held in medical records should be confined to the author and the person clinically responsible for the patient during the episode for which the data has been collected. The clinician can depart from this in the clinical interest of the patient;
- an individual is not to be identifiable from data supplied for statistical or research purposes, except when follow-up of the individual patient is a necessary part of the research and either the patient has given informed consent or consent has been obtained from the chairman of an appropriate ethical committee.

In addition, the Child Health Computing Committee is exploring how data banks can be protected against leakage. One obvious provision is to warn the employees of local authorities with access to the data. It would also seem desirable to acquaint parents with the existence of the Notification of Birth form and to give reasons why information of particular types is required. Further, the Child Health Computing Committee has emphasised the need for a powerful data protection authority.

The BMA has repeatedly expressed concern about DHSS plans to computerise medical records. In late-1981 a series of seminars was arranged for regional health administrators to discuss the findings of the NHS Steering Group on Health Information. The Steering Group developed plans for tests in pilot districts – Exeter, Hereford, Birmingham and the North East – subject to consultation with doctors and administrators. Such plans could lead to the medical records of every hospital patient in England and Wales being stored on computer. The objective would be a comprehensive information system covering everyone going to a hospital for investigation, treatment and operation; and to include psychiatric hospitals, maternity wards and out-patient clinics. The files would carry details of name, date of birth, sex, marital status, address, GP, consultant, whether NHS or private, diagnosis, treatment, ward, etc. All the information would go on the computers at the DHAs, and there would be provision for integrating the patient information with other computerised systems being developed.

The Child Health Computer System is being developed, despite BMA reservations. Dr John Dawson of the BMA observed in late-1981: 'We are still not happy with the way things are going, and we will advise doctors not to do anything until an independent data protection authority has been set up'. It has been suggested that Home Office control over data protection would threaten the traditional independence of doctors.

In 1981 it was reported that confidential BMA records had been leaked to an insurance company. The BMA stores information about its members on a computer that it shares with the Medical Insurance Agency, an organisation that relies on doctors for its business. The medical magazine *Pulse* stated that lists of members, their dates of birth and their current addresses had been made available to the company, and that this information was subsequently used to post special offers to doctors. A former MIA employee was quoted: 'We could, say, get a printout of all BMA doctors in London over 40 and under 65, printed on sticky labels'. A BMA spokesman later declared: 'We are trying to find out whether or not people have had access to the computer . . . We have never knowingly allowed anyone access to it . . . I would think that the MIA put in a written request for the information, and someone didn't think to clear it, but just printed out the list'.

BMA concern has also been expressed about the 1982 UK Government White Paper on data protection (*Data Protection: The Government's Proposals for Legislation*, Cmnd 8539) (see Chapter 4). The BMA considerations are similar, in many ways, to those that bear on the police collection, storage and use of personal information – and the same questions can be asked. What information is collected? What are the intended uses of the information? Can individuals check the information held about them? What are the safeguards to prevent illicit access to the information by unauthorised internal and external people? Who draws up the safeguards and monitors their application?

Computerised medical records, like computerised police records, in principle facilitate access to a vast amount of personal information about citizens. It is easy to indicate the many legitimate uses to which this information can be put, but clearly in certain circumstances it would be possible to use the information in illicit ways that were not in the interest of the individuals in question. Adequate safeguards, through legislation and other means, should be able to protect personal information while allowing legitimate access for medical purposes.

PERSONNEL ADMINISTRATION

Personnel departments are expected to keep files on employees, collecting and storing information which is often highly sensitive. Traditionally such files have been maintained on a manual basis but there is a growing tendency to automate aspects of personnel administration along with other areas of business operation. Companies inevitably vary in the types of employee information that they record but it typically includes details on education, marital status, medical history (where employees are required to undergo a medical examination as a condition of appointment), previous employers, etc. Sometimes an employer will think it necessary to record nationality, religion and any associations or other organisations to which the employee belongs. (It is a common practice for an employer to consult a former employer of a job applicant in order to obtain information about character, suitability for the post in question, and other aspects. And this can and does occur in the absence of the applicant's permission.) Again we may ask what types of information do employers collect? For what purposes? Can the employee check the record? What are the safeguards to prevent unauthorised access?

Personnel work involves a number of functions: eg personnel planning (to ensure that the organisation's manpower needs are met); recruitment and hiring; setting wage and salary levels; general personnel administration (of promotions, safety programmes, grievance procedures, retirement policies, etc); labour relations; and maintaining personnel records. Westin (April 1982) notes that even before computers were used in personnel work it was common for US organisations to record a wide range of information about employees. For example, details were typically collected on:

— *Personal characteristics* (eg name, age, sex, race, marital status, spouse's name, dependants, hair and eye colour, weight, etc);

— *Recruiting and hiring aspects* (including data on job applications, arrests and convictions, employment history, medical history, skills, interests, results of interviews and tests, etc);

— *Work history* (including details of former jobs, salaries, promotions, maternity leaves, warnings, absentee record, performance appraisals, etc);

— *Benefits* (including details of medical and dental coverage, psychiatric services, pensions, stock options, emergency loans, etc);

— *Education and training* (including data on attendance and performance at courses);

— *Skills* (including details of language skills, hobbies, sports, political activities, travel, patents obtained, etc);

— *Health and safety* (including data on medical handicaps, medical checks, screening programmes, whether exposed to dangerous materials, etc).

It has been suggested, at least for the US, that much of the investigation conducted by employers into potential employees in the 1950s and 60s would not be acceptable today. One consequence is that many employers may still hold inappropriate records – which cannot be abandoned or updated without employee participation. In such circumstances there is a strong case for employee access to files. And the question is also raised as to what constitutes 'appropriate' personnel information. Are employers entitled to know about an employee's minor psychiatric treatment, a twenty-year-old criminal conviction, unusual sexual proclivities, etc? Are employers entitled to know what employees do in their leisure time? Should the employer release *any* information about an employee to organisations or individuals outside the company without the employee's permission? Who, within the organisation, should be allowed access to the records?

Concern may also be expressed about how employee information is collected. Usually employees are asked to complete forms or to provide information orally, but personality tests or stress interviews may be used which the employee is unable to evaluate. Should the results be made known to the employee? In some circumstances, deliberately secretive neighbourhood investigations may be carried out to collect data on the lifestyle and character of a job applicant or employee. And employees may be subject to general surveillance by means of hidden listening devices, closed-circuit television monitoring, planted agents, etc. Such matters have clear relevance to the privacy issue.

Most of these areas of concern have a record-keeping aspect. Information is collected and stored to aid management in the supervision of an enterprise. However, it is clear that companies vary in the types of information they collect and the safeguards they deem necessary.

Since the early-1970s increasing use has been made of computer-based systems for personnel administration – leading to the creation of more up-to-date and more detailed records about individuals, faster responses to enquiries about individuals, more extensive manipulation of stored information, and enhanced provisions for exchanging data between branches of an organisation and between one organisation and another. In response to these developments there was increased pressure on managements to allow employees access to their own files, and some companies – notably in the US – have made provision for such access in one way or another. Again, different employers have different attitudes. Westin (January 1982) has noted that three possible positions can be identified as to what should be done in the handling of personnel data by employers:

— *Nothing is required.* Here employee privacy is seen as a non-issue, not requiring any special codes, rules or procedures. Nothing, it is suggested, would be gained by putting managements under further costly information-handling requirements or by restricting further their activities by legislation;

— *Voluntary employer action should be encouraged.* Here fair information-handling procedures can be evolved by employers and expert groups, to be adopted by responsive managements. It is assumed that there *are* necessary principles but that these should not be enforced in law;

— *Some legislation is needed.* It is suggested that experience – in such areas as equal opportunities and safety – does not support the idea of voluntary action. For example, it is pointed out that of the 85,000 US firms of more than 100 employees only a few dozen have adopted the exemplary privacy provisions of such firms as IBM, Bank of America and Ford. On this argument, legislative safeguards are recommended.

INTERNATIONAL DATA FLOWS

A new dimension is added to the privacy question when the international transmission of data* is considered. In such circumstances it is no longer sufficient that one country have adequate data protection safeguards: if information is transmitted from that country to one without adequate safeguards then the information is insecure. Companies in a country with adequate data protection legislation may be reluctant to enter into contracts with firms in a country without such legislation. Such considerations are one of the major pressures forcing the UK Government to consider effective data protection legislation.

Different national attitudes and laws regarding data protection cause difficulties in the international transmission of data. For example, there are significant differences in how protection principles are implemented in the US, Canada and the various European countries. The English may talk about 'protecting people's privacy' whereas the Scandinavian and German-speaking countries focus on the idea of 'data protection'. The French prefer to consider the problem in terms of 'data processing and individual freedom' (*informatique et libertés individuelles*).

In the US there are specific privacy laws governing different private and public sectors, whereas laws in European countries (excluding the UK, Greece and Turkey) are individually expected to cover both sectors. Some European privacy laws only apply to computerised data, but the German Federal Data Protection Law and US legislation cover both computerised and manual data.

* An important journal in this field is *Transnational Data Report*, published by North-Holland in association with Transnational Data Reporting service.

Various European countries, unlike the US, have special data-protection boards or commissions with special staff.

In these circumstances it is obvious that legislative and other differences from one country to another could greatly complicate the interpretation of data protection requirements. Applicable national laws may be in conflict and it may not be obvious which laws of which country apply to a particular situation. The OECD (Organisation for Economic Co-operation and Development, consisting of Western Europe, the US, Canada, Japan, Australia, New Zealand, Greece and Turkey) has prepared guidelines governing the protection of privacy and international flows of personal data. In a 1979 draft the OECD philosophy of the guidelines was expressed: '. . . although national law and policies may differ, member countries have a common interest in protecting privacy and individual liberties, and in reconciling fundamental but competing values such as privacy and the free flow of information.' Furthermore, it was suggested that 'domestic legislation concerning privacy protection and transborder flows of personal data may hinder such transborder flows.'

In addition to OECD activity, the issue of transborder data flows is currently being considered in the Council of Europe (COE), the European Economic Community (EEC), the Nordic Council, and at various conferences sponsored by the United Nations Educational, Scientific and Cultural Organisation (UNESCO) and the Intergovernmental Bureau for Informatics (IBI). Various mechanisms have been proposed to cope with the problems of transborder data flows (TDF). Gelinas (1981), for instance, outlines a mechanism for privacy implementation for the US which could eliminate the problems of TDF between the US and the various European countries. This proposes the development of a privacy audit and report.

Concern has been expressed at the impact on personal privacy of such national and international networks as Euronet, Venus (for Japanese international data transmission), the Nordic Data Network (for Scandinavia), and the ATT scheme for the Advanced Communications Service (ACS). A central question is how much personal data will be handled, stored and transmitted by systems of this sort.

OTHER AREAS

Privacy considerations bear on many other sectors* in society which are moving towards greater implementation of computer-based systems. Typical examples include:

— *banks*: it is important, for example, that electronic funds transfer (EFT) systems include adequate safeguards;

— *electronic mail*: privacy of the mail would clearly be eroded if adequate safeguards were not considered an essential element controlling this type of office system;

— *point-of-sale systems*: consumer transactions, possibly via point-of-sale facilities linked to the consumer's bank, are an obvious area where privacy safeguards are needed;

— *school records*: the increased availability of economic computer-based systems for schools, possibly linked to other computers, has clear implications for data protection.

Such examples, which could easily be extended, serve to illustrate the general point that wherever personal information is stored – in a manual or computerised system – it is necessary to pay attention to data protection considerations. These may variously involve system design features, adequate company codes and procedures for system operation, and appropriate legislation. The aim must be to balance the safeguarding of civil liberties against the efficient functioning of the various necessary social institutions.

SUMMARY

There are many social sectors that bear on the issue of personal privacy. Wherever information is obtained about people – to be stored, retrieved, manipulated, etc – there is a need to look to adequate data protection principles. This is a particularly pressing requirement where considerable power over the private citizen is vested in an organisation (such as government and the police). It has even been suggested (Kling, 1981) that computer abuses can be viewed 'as part of the routine activities of organisations rather than as isolated and dramatic individual actions'.

* It is useful to look at the various sectors examined by the 1978 Lindop Committee (see Chapter 3).

Many of the questions that need to be asked apply equally to the various social sectors – What information is collected? For what purposes? Is it stored securely? Is it accurate? Can the individual check the information?

There is widespread recognition that organisations need some legislative control in their handling of information, though there is debate as to how extensive the legislation should be. The obvious importance of the various areas of concern clearly puts governments under obligation to interest themselves in data protection as a means of safeguarding citizens' rights.

3 Background to UK Legislation

INTRODUCTION

The possibility of effective privacy legislation has been discussed in the UK for well over a decade. In the 1960s many observers expressed concern about the growing capability of computer-based systems to store vast amounts of personal information without adequate safeguards. The need for data protection was recognised but there was disagreement about the proper legislative measures required to accomplish such an objective.

The UK debate on privacy, data protection, system security and related questions was mirrored by similar discussions in other advanced countries – notably the countries of North America and Western Europe. Unlike the UK, however, a number of countries moved to implement national or local data protection legislation, and by 1980 the UK was in a small minority of advanced nations that had failed, for whatever reason, to enact laws designed to protect the growing volume of personal information held in computer-based (and manual) systems.

Throughout the 1970s, successive UK governments were under pressure from various sources to introduce data protection laws. Three sources of such pressure can be identified:

— pressure groups such as computer users, the National Council for Civil Liberties (NCCL) and other interested bodies. Such groups often advanced detailed suggestions for legislation in circumstances where the state was perceived as gaining more and more power over the private citizen;

— individual Members of Parliament prepared to lobby, to encourage debate, and even to draft Bills with a view to enactment;

— detailed reports (eg Younger and Lindop, see below), usually instigated by government, which invariably concluded that new data protection measures were needed but which often differed on the precise measures to be adopted;

— companies concerned that the absence of adequate data protection legislation in the UK may put them at a disadvantage compared with companies operating in countries deemed to have adequate data protection legislation.

The various pressures led to a government White Paper (*Data Protection, The Government's Proposals for Legislation*, Cmnd 8539) which was presented to Parliament in April 1982 (see Chapter 4). It is worth indicating in more detail some of the 1970s pressures. Only in this context is it possible to evaluate the current government proposals and to anticipate what legislative measures may be reasonably anticipated in the future.

EARLY EFFORTS

Highlighting Computer Dangers

In 1972, The National Computing Centre published *Privacy, Computers and You* which included various contributions from experts in the field of privacy and data protection. 'Some Legislative Proposals for the Proper Regulation of Data Banks' advanced by Joseph Jacob (law department, London School of Economics) reflected concerns which had been expressed by the author in an earlier article ('Seven Dangers of Computers', *New Society*, 11/12/69). In that article it was argued that there were various dangers of which the community should be aware:

— 'The greater the quantities of information the state and private organisations acquire about the individual, and the greater the ease with which they are able to manipulate it, the less power (and self respect) the individual will feel he has.'

— 'The mere ability to digest data will itself lead to the acquisition of more.'

— There 'must inevitably' be 'increases in the misuse of information'.

— 'The numbers of (data) banks will be comparatively small.' This means that errors will be magnified.

— 'The more that data of past contact is used, the greater will be the tendency to act not from volition but for the record.'

— 'It is inherent in the operation of any data bank that inaccurate, incomplete and irrelevant information will be stored.'

— 'The collection of statistical information will lead to the substitution of statistics for value judgements.'

In the NCC publication, Joseph Jacob added that there would be 'an over-reliance on the products of computers in the same way as there is an over-reliance on the printed rather than the spoken word.' And furthermore 'a computer's record of an individual can never be more than an identikit of him and it cannot record the dignity of his humanity.' Jacob suggests that an effective data surveillance Act would, amongst other things, aim at:

— giving the individual the power to combat the information holders and so increase his self-respect;

— preventing or limiting the mere ability for the digestion of data leading to a hunger for more;

— limiting information misuse;

— limiting the storage of inaccurate, incomplete or irrelevant information;

— countering the depersonalisation effects of the computerisation of data banks by the direct involvement of the individual with his record.

NCCL Draft Bill

Privacy, Computers and You (NCC, 1972) also includes an NCCL bill (drafted by Jacob) intended to establish a data bank tribunal, to license the operation of data banks containing personal information, to enable the individual to see and correct any stored information and to control its use, and to know the purposes for which such information is used.

The Bill proposes that the Tribunal shall consist of five legally qualified persons and not less than ten other members. The terms under which members are elected to the Tribunal are set out, with considerable powers vested in the Lord Chancellor. The aim is that the Tribunal shall grant licences, 'on such terms and conditions as it may think fit', to those responsible for managing stores of information containing personal details of groups of individuals ('other than his own employees or the employees of any company substantially owned by him'). A list of granted licences shall, under the terms of the Bill, be available for public inspection.

Each licence-holder would be obliged to supply to individuals, about whom information is held, details of such information and also the names and addresses of all persons and organisations to whom the information had been made available since the last time any information was supplied. The information need not be supplied if it relates to criminal matters (eg where disclosure would be detrimental to the detection of crime). Otherwise, this information should be made available to the individual at regular intervals or when the individual makes a specific request.

This Bill empowers the Tribunal to order the erasure or correction of items of information if found to be inaccurate or irrelevant to the purpose for which the information is stored. Various other powers would also be vested in the Tribunal. For example, it would be able to order a licence-holder not to divulge information to specific organisations, and would be able to order licence-holders to pay damages to any person harmed by failure to comply with particular provisions of the Bill. In addition, there would be heavy legal sanctions in certain cases (involving fines, imprisonment or both). The draft Bill has been applauded by many interested observers, though criticisms (eg some looseness in drafting) have also been made.

Kenneth Baker's Data Surveillance Bill (1969)

This Bill was intended 'to prevent the invasion of privacy through the misuse of computer information'. It recommended that a register should be kept, by the Registrar of Restrictive Trading

Agreements, of all data banks operated by (or on behalf of): any agency of government, any public corporation, any person exercising public authority, any person offering to supply information about other people's credit worthiness, any private detective, and any person who offers for sale information stored in a data bank. Under the terms of this Bill, the owner of the data bank is obliged to give his/her name and address, the name and address of the person responsible for its operation, and the location of the data bank. The person responsible for its operation is required to register any required technical details, the nature of the stored data (and of data to be stored), the purpose of the data, and the 'class of persons' who have access to it.

The Registrar is given powers to expunge items from the register, 'guided by the principle that only data relevant to the purposes for which the data bank is operated should be stored therein, and that such data should only be disclosed for those same purposes'. The register is to be open to inspection by the public, 'provided that entries relating to data banks operated by the police, the security services and the armed forces shall be kept in a separate part of the register which shall not be open to inspection by the public'. The operator of each data bank is required to record in writing the date of each extraction of data, who requested the data, and the nature and purpose of the supplied data – unless the data bank in question:

— does not contain personal information relating to identifiable persons;

— is operated by the police;

— is operated by the security services;

— is operated by the armed forces.

Apart from such exceptions, individuals about whom information is stored 'shall receive from the operator, not later than two months after his name is first programmed into the data bank, a printout of all the data contained therein which relates to him'. Thereafter, printouts should be made available on request ('upon payment of a fee the amount of which shall be determined by the Registrar from time to time'). A statement, detailing the uses to which the data has been put and the names and addresses of the recipients of the data, shall accompany each printout. If an individual detects incorrect data he may appeal to the Registrar to order its removal from the data bank. The Bill allows for penal sanctions (fines, imprisonment or both) to be variously applied to the owner and operator of the data bank if there is failure to register the data bank, failure to provide a printout when required to do so, if data is used for purposes other than those stated on the register, if people other than those stated on the register are allowed access, or if there is failure to comply with a decision of the Registrar.

Brian Walden's Privacy Bill (1969)

This Bill was introduced on 26th November 1969 in the House of Commons 'to establish a right of privacy, to make consequential amendments to the law of evidence, and for connected purposes'. Two earlier bills of this type had been presented – one in the Lords (1961), and one in the Commons (1967). The government reacted to the Walden initiative by setting up the (Younger) Committee on Privacy with these terms of reference: 'To consider whether legislation is needed to give further protection to the individual citizen and to commercial and industrial interests against intrusions into privacy by private persons and organisations, or by companies, and to make recommendations' (see The Younger Report, below).

The Walden Bill takes 'right of privacy' to mean the right of any person to be protected from intrusion upon himself, his home, his family, his relationships and communications with others, his property and his business affairs. Consideration is given to various means of intrusion:

— spying, prying, watching or besetting;
— the unauthorised overhearing or recording of spoken words;
— the unauthorised reading or copying of documents;
— the unauthorised use or disclosure of confidential information, or of facts calculated to cause him distress, annoyance or embarrassment, or to place him in a false light;
— the unauthorised appropriation of his name, identity or likeness for another's gain.

It is declared that any 'substantial and unreasonable infringement' of the right of privacy 'shall be actionable at the suit of any person whose right of privacy has been so infringed; and that the defendant in such an action may be a person who has committed the infringement, a person who has been party to it, or a person who, knowing of the infringement, has made use of it. (In due course, fourteen members of the Younger Committee were to reject the idea of such legislation, with two in favour of it.)

Leslie Huckfield's Personal Information Bill (1971)

The second of Joseph Jacob's NCCL draft bills was adopted by Huckfield in introducing his Control of Personal Information Bill. This was devised 'to establish a data bank tribunal and inspectorate; to provide for the licensing of data banks containing personal information; and to make other provisions to prevent the misuse of information stored in data banks'. The Huckfield Bill, not surprisingly, is similar to the original NCCL draft bill, already considered. A difference in the second NCCL draft is the emphasis given to the appointment of a chief inspector of data banks.

Once appointed, under the terms of the Bill, the chief inspector of data banks shall appoint other inspectors 'and servants' as he deems necessary. The chief inspector shall report to the Tribunal regarding any failure to obtain a licence, any failure to comply with conditions set by the Tribunal, or with subsequent orders made by the Tribunal once the Act is established. Any shortcomings in stored data, violations of the Act, etc, shall be reported to the Tribunal by the chief inspector (and by any other appointed inspectors).

This Bill also stipulates the size of data bank which is intended to be governed by the legislation. Data banks containing details of individuals 'numbering over one hundred thousand persons' are required to operate under licences granted by the Tribunal (and the wording of this section allows that a person may operate *a number* of data banks which collectively contain details of more than one hundred thousand individuals). A person in the UK who frequently uses a data bank 'situated in whole or in part' outside the UK is also subject to the Act.

The Huckfield Bill represents a serious effort to provide effective legislation for data protection. It is significant in proposing an inspectorate to support the role of the Tribunal. As with the other proposed bills, the Huckfield measures were never enacted.

THE YOUNGER REPORT

The Younger Committee on Privacy was in existence from 13th May 1970 to 25th May 1972. The governments responsible (ie the Labour Government which appointed the Committee and the Conservative Government which took office before it seriously started work) clearly admitted the importance of the privacy question, though the terms of reference of the Committee's investigation were severely limited; eg to the private sector.

The composition of the Younger Committee was only decided after much discussion. Some people who were approached declined to serve because of the limitations on the terms of reference. The NCCL was not invited to attend, a circumstance seen by some as 'a most curious omission' (eg Madgwick and Smythe, 1974). Two women were invited to serve: Mrs Kathleen Evans, a Justice of the Peace, was joined after ten months by novelist Margaret Drabble. The enquiry dealt with privacy in general: only a relatively small part focused on the implications of computer-based systems.

An initial difficulty was to clarify the terms of reference. It was significant that much of the pressure for privacy protection was occasioned by the activities of public sector bodies, in particular the intrusive practices of Government departments. Difficulties emerged in connection with the BBC and ITA (later the IBA), local authorities, universities and the computerisation of personal records. When doubts were put to Mr Callaghan, he commented on 5th June 1970 that the Government would not extend the terms of reference to cover local authorities or public corporations as these were already governed by statute and they were answerable, either directly or indirectly, to the electorate. At the same time, the Government expressed interest in working out a code of conduct for the use of Government-owned computers. On the 23rd July, following the change of Government, Mr Maudling reaffirmed Mr Callaghan's comments on the exclusion of the public sector (Madgwick and Smythe: 'It would no more occur to either of them to put the whole public sector under public scrutiny than it would occur to a magician to reveal the secrets of the Magic Circle').

The Committee invited the submission of evidence by, in part, advertising in forty-four national and regional newspapers. Letters were sent to organisations deemed to have particular interest in privacy matters: at first, such organisations totalled 142, later rising to 225 when suggestions from various other quarters were received. The relatively small response from the public at large was not held to vitiate the need for action in this field: it was, for example, pointed out that most invasions of privacy took place in secret and would not, by their nature, be known to the individuals concerned.

The privacy aspects investigated by the Younger Committee fell into five categories:

— unwanted publicity: (a) Press, (b) broadcasting;

— misuse of personal information: (a) credit rating agencies, (b) banks, (c) employment, (d) students and teachers, and (e) medicine;

— intrusion on home life: (a) prying by neighbours, landlords and others, (b) sales and promotional methods, (c) private detectives, and (d) noise;

— intrusion in business life: industrial espionage;

— modern technical developments: (a) technical surveillance devices, and (b) computers.

One initial problem in investigating these aspects was that the Committee had difficulty in defining the concept of privacy – 'no useful purpose would be served by our also entering the lists with yet another attempt to formulate a precise and comprehensive definition of privacy'. In these circumstances, the next task 'is to try to decide what are the values in which privacy is a major element, and then to decide which deserve protection'. It was, however, felt that a right of privacy under the law should not be synonymous with a right to be let alone (which was 'an unrealistic concept, incompatible with the concept of society'). Instead, 'the type of conduct against which legal protection might be afforded on the ground of intrusion of privacy should be confined to injurious or annoying conduct deliberately aimed at a particular person or persons where the invasion of privacy is the principal wrong complained of'.

The small section of the Younger Report that dealt with computers received a mixed response. Madgwick and Smythe, for instance, with their strong civil rights focus, saw this part of the report as one of its weakest sections – 'the Committee seemed curiously unaware of the very *nature* of the problem . . .' (original italics), failing to recognise that most of the victims of data bank abuse do not know that their privacy is being violated. At the same time the Committee stated (in the early-1970s):

> 'In a few years time from now, it may be technically possible for details of your life, such as family circumstances, financial situation, political views and so on to be recorded on a big central computer, with any of the information being available to anyone who asks for it.'

A public response to this statement may be taken as highly significant: 87 per cent declared that they would regard it as an invasion of privacy, with 85 per cent believing that such a state of affairs should be prohibited by law. At the same time the Committee was prepared to state that 'So far as the protection of privacy is concerned, most problems are common to all data banks, whether computerised or not'. With regard to computers alone, the Younger Report makes the following recommendations for immediate *voluntary* adoption by computers users:

1) Information should be regarded as held for a specific purpose and not be used, without appropriate authorisation, for other purposes.

2) Access to information should be confined to those authorised to have it for the purpose for which it was supplied.

3) The amount of information collected and held should be the minimum necessary for the achievement of the specified purpose.

4) In computerised systems handling information for statistical purposes, adequate provision should be made in their design and programs for separating identities from the rest of the data.

5) There should be arrangements whereby the subject could be told about the information held concerning him.

6) The level of security to be achieved by a system should be specified in advance by the user and should include precautions against the deliberate abuse or misuse of information.

7) A monitoring system should be provided to facilitate the detection of any violation of the security system.

8) In the design of information systems, periods should be specified beyond which the information should not be retained.

9) Data held should be accurate. There should be machinery for the correction of inaccuracy and the updating of information.

10) Care should be taken in coding value judgements.

A final recommendation is that the Government 'should consider the possibility' of extending the enquiry to the public sector. This point was welcomed by most observers: they were less keen on the *voluntarism* implicit in the Committee's broad recommendations, preferring to emphasise the need for *enforcement* of the necessary conditions.

The Younger Report has been represented as giving too little attention to computers, and as focusing too extensively on the voluntary implementation of the recommendations. To a large extent, however, it prepared the ground for the Lindop investigation.

THE LINDOP REPORT

General

In 1975 the UK Government announced in a White Paper* its intention to prepare legislation to set out the standards governing the use of computers that process personal information and to establish a statutory data protection authority to oversee the use of computers with regard to privacy. A Data Protection Committee, chaired by Sir Norman Lindop, was appointed to advise on the legislation. It is noted in the Data Protection White Paper (Cmnd

* *Computer and Privacy*, Cmnd 6353, and its supplement, *Computers: Safeguards for Privacy*, Cmnd 6354.

8539) of April 1982 that the Lindop Report (Cmnd 7341) 'contains very helpful background information and a valuable analysis of ways of overcoming the problems involved'. (Lindop has no idea why he was chosen as Younger's successor. When he pointed out to the Home Office that he had no special interest in, or knowledge of, data protection he was told that this was 'neither a disadvantage nor a disqualification'.)

An initial task of the Lindop Committee, as with Younger, was to explore the meaning of 'privacy'. The Committee favoured the term 'data privacy' to mean 'the individual's claim to control the circulation of data about himself' – following the definitions provided by Professor Alan Westin in *Privacy and Freedom* ('Privacy is the claim of individuals, groups or institutions to determine for themselves when, how and to what extent information about them is communicated to others') and Professor Arthur Miller in *Assault on Privacy* ('the individual's ability to control the circulation of information relating to him'). In contrast with Younger, the Lindop Committee considered privacy in connection with computerised information systems – 'in the sense of information systems which include, as one of their elements, some processing by automatic means'.

Chapter 3 ('The Impact of Technology on Data Protection') of the Lindop Report explores the character of information systems and their impact ('By the time the Younger Committee was appointed, the existence of many very large computerised personal information systems had begun to become a matter of concern . . . Since then however . . . the pace of developments in technology has accelerated'). The Lindop Committee received written evidence from such computing organisations as The National Computing Centre, the British Computer Society, and the Data Processing Management Association. Practical demonstrations of operational systems were arranged, and during a visit to Stockholm several government and commercial systems were seen in operation. To aid familiarisation with the prevailing technical terminology, advice was offered by members of the Civil Service Department's Central Computer Agency and by the Managing Director of IBM Laboratories, Hursley. The Committee noted the rapid development of computer technology with computing becoming 'far more ubiquitous and less remote'.

Areas of Interest

Following a discussion of the international scene (with focus on the then current legislation and regulation provisions), individual chapters deal with current computerised personal information practices in various UK sectors. These include:

— *Central Government.* This section includes discussion of the possibility of transferring personal information between central government departments. It is pointed out (for 1978) that, for example, the systems dealing with National Insurance, Pensions and Child Allowances hold 48 million records, that the Department of National Savings handles about 10 million accounts, that the Department of Education carries the records of 3.5 million students, and that the Office of Population Censuses* and Surveys aims to collect information about every individual in the country. The Committee also describes here the relevant activities of the Inland Revenue, the Department of Employment, the Department of Health and Social Security, the Civil Service Department, and some aspects of the Home Office (other aspects are considered elsewhere);

— *National Health Service.* The NHS records contain detailed personal information about nearly everyone in the country, though, as we have seen, there is no totally comprehensive computerised system in the UK. The type and purpose of patient records are described, and attention is given to such aspects as the Community Health Register and Recall System, the confidentiality of patients' records ('safeguarded by the ethics of the medical and dental professions'), the ownership of medical records, the Hospital Activity Analysis, the Mental Health Enquiry, the Oxford Record Linkage Study, and the extent of patient access to medical records (Alfred Morris, the then Under-Secretary of State for Health and Social Security, suggested in 1976 that 'The decision whether or not to disclose information [from medical records] to anybody, including the patient himself, is one which involves clinical judgement');

* The Government requirement for census information has often aroused public concern over privacy questions.

— *Police and Security Services.* This sector constituted a 'relatively small part' of the Committee's work. It is noted that 'most of the evidence . . . received from the police was helpful and willingly given, but the Metropolitan Police seemed to assume that a wide exemption would be granted for police applications . . .'. The Association of Chief Police Officers expressed concern at the number of computer-based facilities not wholly operated by the police themselves. Several officers are concerned that sensitive information (eg criminal information) should not be held on a system shared with a local authority or some other non-police body. Details are given in this chapter about the Police National Computer, the Metropolitan Police computer system for criminal intelligence, police access to the records of other organisations, and the extent to which national security systems should be exempt from consideration. (It was claimed, for instance, by the Northern Ireland Civil Rights Association that the Army in Ulster had computer records on up to 40 per cent of the population of Ulster, and that the Army used its powers of arrest and interrogation under the Emergency Provisions Act to update its files);

— *Local Government.* It is noted that local government services cover education, housing, social services, police, fire brigades, town and country planning, public transport, highways, leisure services, environmental health and consumer protection. Such wide-ranging activities necessarily involve the collection and use of a vast amount of information. In considering evidence from local authorities, a lack of consensus was observed among the witnesses ('. . . policies and practices about privacy varied between local authorities, and . . . the arrangements in some authorities would be regarded by others as abusing confidentiality or security'). Attention is given in this chapter to the LAMSAC Report (*Computer Privacy: Notes of Guidance for Local Authorities*), social work records, and the wide impact of local government activities (it is pointed out that 'local government comes closer to the lives of ordinary people than any other body in the public or private sector');

— *Nationalised Industries*. These are seen as sharing most of the common features of private industrial and commercial organisations. To a degree they are controlled by government, but matters such as the use of computers are within their own control. Evidence was obtained from the Nationalised Industries Computer Committee and from several of the industries independently. Specifically, the Lindop Committee considers British Airways, the Electricity Supply Industry, and other nationalised industries. It is noted that the then Post Office operated more than 250 computers (the Report discusses data handling activities, the monitoring of information passing over Post Office telecommunications equipment, agency service computer applications, and the National Data Processing Service). The then Post Office, a major user of computers, was highly conscious of the threat to privacy which they present;

— *Education*. The education process requires that detailed records be kept about pupils and students. Evidence on such matters was provided by the Department of Education, the Headmasters' Association, the National Union of Teachers, the Universities Central Council on Admissions, and the Open University. The Committee considered such specific aspects as student records, the Universities Statistical Record, and the Further Education Statistical Record;

— *Employment*. Most organisations need to maintain detailed staff records, both for pay accounting and taxation purposes, and for personnel management. The National Computing Centre showed that (in December 1977) there were 3332 payroll and 1005 personnel computer applications in operation, representing almost 20 per cent of all the personal information applications on the NCC index. The Lindop Committee considers the earlier Younger findings, and then focuses on the evidence supplied by the Trades Union Congress, individual trade unions, employers, and the NCCL. A similarity is noted between the Younger and Lindop findings for this sector;

— *Credit and Credit Reporting*. This concerns credit grantors and credit reference agencies. The Committee considered such aspects as credit control, the Consumer Credit Act 1974, other types of records relating to credit and debit, and the register of County Court judgments. It is suggested that 'information practices in this field are particularly liable to create risks to privacy';

— *Banking*. Evidence was provided by the British Bankers' Association, the Bank of England, credit card companies, and individual banking organisations. Committee members visited the Skandinaviska Enskilda Banken (Scandinavian Bank Ltd) and the Swedish Bankers' Association. Attention was given to stock registration schemes, existing legislation and other aspects. It was concluded, following Younger, that computers in banking did not change the form of the threat to privacy, only the degree;

— *Insurance*. Insurance companies need to obtain a great deal of personal information, much of it 'particularly private and sensitive'. Also, the industry has arrangements for sharing some information in order to protect itself against fraud. One insurance company was found to be handling more than 10 million policies on a computer-based system. Evidence was provided by the British Insurance Association, the British Insurance Brokers' Association, the Faculty of Actuaries (Scotland), the Life Offices' Association, and other bodies;

— *Building Societies*. The Building Societies Association provided substantial evidence on the use of computers in this field. It was estimated that 90 per cent of all accounts were held on computer. The Committee considered the sources of information about mortgage applicants, confidentiality and disclosure of customer information, and other aspects;

— *Direct Marketing*. This involves sending unsolicited advertising material through the post – a practice seen by some as an intrusion on their privacy. Furthermore, it may entail the linking of information, from various sources, about the purchases, and the personal and financial circumstances of large numbers of people. And it is also possible for direct mail marketing firms to obtain information from other firms about the various transactions they have had with their customers. This usually occurs without the customer's knowledge.

Later in the Lindop Report, 'areas of special concern' are discussed in the context of judgment as to what is necessary for a balance between the privacy of the individual and the legitimate needs of those institutions which serve the individual. The areas considered in this section include:

— the police and the security services;
— medical and social work records;
— employment and education records;
— statistics, research and archives;
— transborder data flows;
— data handling bureaux;
— a universal personal identifier.

Principal Legislative Recommendations

The Lindop Report lists a number of main proposals for a Data Protection Act, and gives specific recommendations for a proposed Data Protection Authority (DPA). Following an explanation of the scope of the statute (defining such terms as 'personal data' and 'automatic handling'), various statutory duties, principles and criteria are presented. For instance, data subjects ('any individual to whom data relate, or can be related') should know what information about them is held, why it is held and who will use it. Data subjects should be able to check that information is accurate, and that only relevant data is used for the defined purpose.

The DPA should draft specific Codes of Practice for the various classes of personal data handling applications, with most applications being covered by a small number of Codes. Where an application belongs to a special class of its own, a special Code should be drafted. The various Codes of Practice should take the form of subsidiary legislation and acquire the force of law.

A scheme of registration is recommended, with a degree of discretion assigned to the DPA over its timing and extent. All the personal data handling applications of central and local government should be called in by the DPA for registration, and in the industrial and private sectors, the Authority should be able to determine when considering a Code of Practice whether or not the registration of all users whose applications are governed by the Code is necessary or helpful. The register – showing sufficient and updated particulars of each registered application, which Code of Practice applies, and certain other information – should be accessible to the public. Parts of the register (where, for example, disclosure could hinder the detection of crime) should, at the discretion of the DPA, not be open to public inspection.

Recommendations are also made on consultation (by the DPA when proposing to draft a Code of Practice), criminal sanctions, ancillary powers for the DPA, and provisions for hearings (if an important disagreement arises between the DPA and any person or body about a Code of Practice). The constitution of the DPA is recommended, including details of composition, the charging of fees, provision for appeals against the DPA, and other aspects.

It is recognised that the Secretary of State should have power to grant exemptions from the purview of the DPA, but this power 'should be precisely limited to national security'. The Report declares that 'police records, including criminal intelligence records, having no bearing on national security should not be exempted'. Furthermore, the DPA should have 'at least one senior official with a security clearance sufficient to enable him to operate in effect as a privacy consultant to the Home Office and the security services, and to work out with them the appropriate rules and safeguards for their systems'. And specific recommendations are made in connection with medical, social work, employment, statistical and research applications; and in connection with transborder data flows and data handling bureaux.

The Lindop report claims to have advanced a scheme 'which would reassure those handling data that protection for data privacy could be provided on a sensible and flexible basis imposing no unreasonable or arduous constraints on data users'. All the Committee members signed the Report, with one member adding a note of reservation.

THE POST-LINDOP SCENE

To some extent the Lindop Report followed the 1975 White Paper, *Computers and Privacy* (Cmnd 6353). The Lindop Codes of Practice centre on an independent Data Protection Authority (DPA) encompassing both the role of ombudsman, handling complaints, and that of a registration authority setting out rules and regulations for computer users. The White Paper suggested these functions as alternative roles for a DPA. The Lindop Report proposed that the DPA should carry out both, and that the Codes of Practice would be flexible enough for each group or organisation using computers to store personal information to be catered for on an individual basis and not under a blanket approach.

The Government response to the Report was ambivalent. Lindop himself has commented that 'The Government at the time was incredibly cagey', and recalled that the then Minister of State observed that 'this animal had an awful lot of teeth'. In 1981, Timothy Raison, Minister of State at the Home Office, gave reasons (quoted in *Computing*, 22/10/81) for rejecting what he called the 'objectionable' DPA recommended by Lindop:

> 'The fact is [Lindop's] Codes of Practice were in reality major extensions of the criminal law, creating a whole host of new offences. We do not believe it is desirable to enlarge the criminal law in this way. We do not think it is constitutionally right to confer responsibility for drafting a whole sector of the criminal law on an independent authority, or that the proposed procedures would be acceptable. Nor do we believe that an independent authority would have the competence to undertake a task which is essentially one for government and Parliament.'

The post-Lindop scene has been marked by a certain tardiness in government in moving to implement legislation on data protection. The seeming slowness in this area has irritated many organisations – including civil liberties groups, computer users and even some sections of government (such as the Department of Industry). Lindop has suggested that *1984* 'is a good deal nearer now than when the report came out', and he suggests reasons why the Home Office has shown apparent lack of impetus in this field.

The Home Office, Lindop suggests, has gathered a lot of information itself, and is not convinced that there is sufficient evidence of abuse of personal information. And there is also the question of cost: effective data protection may be expensive. Lindop continues to press for legislation, though officially relieved of his role of spokesman for the Data Protection Committee in 1978.

Today, four years after the Lindop Report, the situation has changed dramatically, not least because of the colossal impact of microprocessor-based systems. Relatively cheap systems, with vast storage capabilities, can be acquired by users: it is no longer only the large companies and departments of government that can afford large-scale data processing. With the proliferation of computers in modern society it may be difficult to implement effective privacy control measures. Many small systems will, by their nature, be concerned with personal information relating to one's business, domestic activities, correspondence, etc. One observer (Samet, 1982) has commented: 'There is not the slightest chance that the purchasers of such systems will follow the principles enunciated by Lindop and Younger, except perhaps occasionally by accident. Law enforcement on this scale is a non-starter'.

The Government has declared that it intends to legislate for data protection, though there is still some uncertainty about precisely when this will occur. One feeling is that legislation is more likely to follow Younger than Lindop (with its 'awful lot of teeth'), but will focus on the storage of information in computer-based systems rather than information storage by whatever means (a recent NCCL statement emphasised the need to consider both computer-based and manual methods of storing information).

It is clear that there is growing pressure on the UK Government to implement effective legislation in this field, with much of the pressure occurring by virtue of Britain's membership of the European Economic Community. Government plans, and the wide-ranging response to them, are indicated in Chapter 4. The White Paper (Cmnd 8539) in which these plans are outlined acknowledges the relevance of both Younger and Lindop, and also of the data protection Convention adopted by the Council of Europe.

THE EUROPEAN CONVENTION

The Convention on Data Protection*, adopted by the Council of

* *The Convention for the Protection of Individuals with regard to Automatic Processing of Personal Data*

Europe, was opened for signature in January 1981 and was signed by the United Kingdom in May of that year. (Some observers have suggested that the Convention clearly shows Britain to be out-of-line with a number of its European trading partners.) The UK also endorsed, in September 1981, guidelines on privacy protection and transborder data flows drawn up by the Organisation for Economic Co-operation and Development (OECD). Both the Convention and the Guidelines are appended to the April (1982) White Paper.

The Convention (Article 5) requires that 'personal data undergoing automatic processing' shall be obtained and processed fairly and lawfully, shall only be stored and used for specified and legitimate purposes, shall be adequate and not excessive for such purposes, shall be accurate and kept up-to-date, and shall be preserved in a form which allows identification of the data subjects for no longer than is required for the specified purpose. It is further declared (Article 6), that 'personal data revealing racial origin, political opinions or religious or other beliefs, as well as personal data concerning health or sexual life, may not be processed automatically unless domestic law provides appropriate safeguards'; and furthermore this shall also apply to personal data relating to criminal convictions.

A number of additional safeguards are also provided for the individual (Article 8). Thus any person 'shall be enabled:

a) to establish the existence of an automated data file, its main purposes, as well as the identity and habitual residence or principal place of business of the controller of the file;

b) to obtain at reasonable intervals and without excessive delay or expense confirmation of whether personal data relating to him are stored in the automated data file as well as communication to him of such data in an intelligible form;

c) to obtain, as the case may be, rectification or erasure of such data if these have been processed contrary to the provisions of domestic law giving effect to the basic principles set out in Articles 5 and 6 of this convention;

d) to have a remedy if a request for confirmation or, as the case may be, communication, rectification or erasure as referred to in paragraphs b and c of this article is not complied with'.

Derogation from the provisions of Articles 5, 6 and 8 is to be allowed as a 'necessary measure in a democratic society' in the interests of State security, public safety, the monetary interests of the State, the suppression of criminal offences, the protection of the individual, and the protection of the rights and freedoms of others*. Further exemptions may be provided in law in cases where data is used for statistics or for scientific research purposes 'when there is obviously no risk of an infringement of the privacy of the data subjects'.

The Parties to the Convention, when it enters into force, undertake to establish 'appropriate sanctions and remedies for violations of provisions of domestic law giving effect to the basic principles for data protection' set out in Chapter II of the Convention. Eight European countries (Austria, France, Denmark, Iceland, Luxembourg, Norway, Sweden and the Federal Republic of Germany) have now enacted data protection legislation, with others (including Finland, the Netherlands and Switzerland) about to introduce legislative proposals. Eleven countries (Austria, Denmark, France, Luxembourg, Norway, Sweden, Turkey, the Federal Republic of Germany, Portugal, the United Kingdom and Spain) have signed the Council of Europe Convention, but so far none has ratified it. The Convention will only come into force when it has been ratified by a minimum of five states.

SUMMARY

Efforts to encourage successive UK governments to introduce effective data protection legislation have now been made for well over a decade. Appropriate Bills have been drafted and sponsored by Members of Parliament, and two major reports – Younger (on privacy in general, with only a relatively small section dealing with computerised systems) and Lindop (focusing on the protection of data held in computer-based systems) – have been completed.

Pressures for legislation have grown throughout the 1970s and early-1980s, not least from companies who feel that their international trading position will be increasingly hampered by non-existent or inadequate national data protection legislation. Other

* Some observers may feel that this list of exemptions provides governments with excessive latitude.

pressures derive from growing anxiety about the power of the State in the light of rapid and far-reaching technological developments.

The European scene is mixed. Some countries have introduced national data protection laws, but none has yet ratified the Council of Europe Convention. Proposals for legislation, in countries where it has not yet been enacted, are being subjected to detailed scrutiny and some criticism. The UK Government proposals, for instance, as set out in the recent White Paper (Cmnd 8539), appear to satisfy few observers. It is one thing to move to legislation, but quite another to ensure that the eventual legislation satisfies those individuals and organisations it is intended to protect while safeguarding the necessary and legitimate activities of the State and other social institutions.

4 Current UK Proposals

INTRODUCTION

The issue of data protection has become a long-running saga. From the time of the early concerns expressed in the 1960s to the present day, we have witnessed a procession of draft parliamentary bills, reports and recommendations. Repeatedly, observers in various national sectors have expressed impatience with apparent Government reluctance to move to effective legislation in this area. The UK Government has now expressed a commitment to introduce data protection legislation in the near future, with legislative proposals outlined in a White Paper (see below). This chapter profiles some of the reactions to the Government intentions.

PRESSURES FOR LEGISLATION

We have already surveyed (Chapter 3) some of the pressures on Government for legislation in the field of data protection. Some of the pressures derive from the Government's own growing sensitivity to the possibilities inherent in Information Technology (IT). In 1980 the Government announced changes in the Civil Service aimed at coordinating IT policies, at bringing together the technologies of computing, microelectronics and communications. Pressures for a new approach to Information Technology came from the Department of Industry (DoI), from an IT study published by the Advisory Council for Applied Research and Development (ACARD), and from various other sources, including elements of the computer industry. These pressures were often linked to an expressed concern for the need for new data protection legislation.

Senior civil servants in the Department of Industry had expressed impatience with the Home Office for not implementing the various recommendations in the Lindop Report. (When the Report was first published in 1978, the Home Office, then Labour, decided to submit it for comment to the people who spoke to the Lindop Committee. This took another six months, during which time the Government changed.) The 1980 ACARD report on IT reflected some of the impatience about the Government's seeming lack of urgency on data protection legislation. The report declared that 'the lack of data protection legislation will place the UK increasingly at a disadvantage with other countries'. It was stated that 'British commercial and industrial interests will suffer'. In 1980 it seemed likely that the Department of Industry and ACARD would be able to influence the Government through a committee created in the Cabinet Office to coordinate the social, legal and industrial implications of the emerging IT policies.

Many of the pressures continued to have a civil rights rather than a commercial focus. NCCL continued to maintain that data protection legislation was needed to safeguard the rights of the individual, rather than as mainly protecting the profits of companies in the international marketplace. This type of emphasis was reflected in the computer press: for instance, in *Computerworld UK* (11/2/81) it is stated that 'The reason why we need privacy legislation is that the rights of the individual should be respected and given protection in law'. This is seen as 'reason enough', with other arguments (including the risk to commercial interests) only serving 'to cloud the issue'. At the same time there is recognition that UK business may be at risk.

Some parliamentary pressures have consisted in trying to amend new legislation, rather than in urging the need for a specific data protection Act. Ian Mikardo, for instance, MP for Bethnal Green, sought to add an amendment to the Telecommunications Bill to guarantee a measure of data protection. He later withdrew the amendment after being told that the Government was considering the matter urgently.

In March 1981 the Home Secretary, William Whitelaw, promised national legislation 'when the opportunity offers', but at that time offered no timetable; in May 1981 Britain signed the Council of Europe's Convention on Data Protection. At about the same time, the Law Society called for a Green Paper on privacy, and Sir Norman Lindop again criticised the Government for inactivity in the area of data protection. The Law Commission issued a report urging the Government to make abuse of confidential information held in computerised systems a civil law offence. One aim is to put pressure, not only on someone who steals confidential information, but also on someone who receives it, to keep it secret. 'Improper' (though not necessarily illegal) circumstances would include 'unauthorised use of or interference with a computer or similar device in which data is stored'. With these provisions, the obligation of confidence would not apply to a police officer or security official who obtained information lawfully in connection with national security or the prevention of crime.

The British Computer Society, in June 1981, proposed a Data Certification Board to 'police' data banks, again reflecting the anxiety that without privacy laws British companies will be restricted in trading with countries such as Sweden which already have effective legislation. The BCS represented the Data Certification Board as a self-financing organisation of computer professionals that would issue certificates to computer users when their systems had been inspected and seen to comply with privacy codes of practice. With this arrangement the Home Secretary would be given the power to tell individuals, companies and government departments that they must obtain certificates. (By this time the Government had already rejected the main recommendation of the Lindop Report, the creation of a statutory Data Protection Authority with wide powers.)

In February 1982 the *Sun* newspaper printed disclosures about the efforts of a firm of private detectives to gain access to purportedly private information about Michael Meacher (Labour MP for Oldham West). This exercise was carried out to illustrate the point behind Mr Meacher's own private member's Bill, designed to set up an independent authority to license data banks, to establish a code of practice for their operation, and to guarantee public access to individual files.

The detectives apparently uncovered a considerable amount of information about Mr Meacher, much of it only available from police and government computer banks. The firm of detectives, under the impression that the individual was under investigation because he was being considered for a top management consultancy post, charged in excess of £500 for the information (the payment included £362.50 requested because Mr Meacher was an MP). In the House of Commons, the Prime Minister expressed her distaste that personal information should be accessible in this way and promised action to protect personal data stored in computerised systems ('We do regard legislation as urgent. I would hope it will come forward in the next session of Parliament').

GOVERNMENT INTENTIONS

Mr Timothy Raison, Minister of State at the Home Office, speaking to the Parliamentary Information Technology Committee (Pitcom) on 8th June 1981, made clear that a main consequence of the Government's proposed legislation on data protection would be a public register of computer systems handling personal information. At the same time he declared that the Government saw no need for a statutory body (such as the Data Protection Authority proposed in the Lindop Report).

The objective would be legislation to establish a basic framework. Minimum standards would be stated for all systems, and for each group of systems a designation order would be brought in, imposing the obligation to register and providing the specific code designed for that group of systems. In order to secure registration, information would have to be given regarding the system type, its purpose, who is to use it, the system's electronic and physical security features, details of data quality maintenance, and how accessible the stored information is to data subjects.

Safeguards would be made for especially sensitive information (such as that relating to race, religion and politics), and there would be special provision for police and national security systems. There would be some scope for discretion on how the minimum standards were realised, but organisations would be bound by what they publicly declared at the time of registration (Raison: 'If the statutory principles permitted it in the special circumstances of a particular case an operator could refuse all access or observe only quite limited standards in respect of the quality of information').

Consultations would take place on legislation and on the standards to be set for each group of systems. Designation orders would be brought in over a period of time and would be subject to review in appropriate circumstances.

Such a scheme would include, for the private sector, the provision that failure to register would be a criminal offence. The public sector would be controlled by the ombudsman. Mr Raison recognised that these proposals represented 'a fairly limited level of enforcement', justified by the limited evidence of abuse and the difficulties in establishing effective control in a complex area. No timetable for legislation was indicated at the Pitcom meeting.

A central element in Government thinking, as expressed throughout much of 1981, was to make the Home Office act as its own watchdog on the use of personal data stored in computerised systems. (This idea was modified, to some extent, in 1982.) Hostility was expressed to the Lindop idea of an independent Data Protection Authority, and there was not much Government enthusiasm for the BCS idea of a Data Certification Board (Raison suggested that the BCS scheme could form a voluntary system complementary to the statutory framework but expressed concern about costs and about whether the proposals would command general support).

In September 1981, Mr Raison, addressing the British Medical Association's data protection conference, stated that 'The independent authority proposed by Sir Norman's committee is fundamentally objectionable', pointing out that it would create a host of new offences and that it was not desirable to enlarge the criminal law in this way. Instead, the Home Office would be designated as the responsible body ('As I am only too well aware, we shall be subject to parliamentary and public scrutiny in a way which would not apply to a non-accountable body').

Mr Raison has further suggested that the Government proposals would comply with the Council of Europe's Data Protection Convention. The European Commission has recommended that member States be required to ratify the Convention by the end of 1982. A provision of the Convention is that a country must have data protection legislation in order to ratify. Clearly this represents further pressure on the UK Government to enact suitable legislation.

By February 1982 concern was being expressed in various quarters about the scope of the data protection plans to be set out in the impending White Paper. One fear was that, although the move away from sole Home Office responsibility was welcome, the White Paper would propose no more than a single guardian without the powers to inspect Home Office files, and without the resources to effectively control private data banks. A system of voluntary controls was anticipated, watched over by an independent registrar. Michael Meacher tabled a question in the House of Commons asking how many staff would be employed and what they would do. This underlines the fear that the registrar is likely to be a solitary figure ('drawn from the ranks of the great and the good' – Veitch, 11/2/82), with inadequate resources to investigate complaints against the Home Office which, after all, controls a vast range of sensitive computer files.

Mr Raison claimed that the independent registrar 'would be appointed by the Government, but would be independent in the exercise of his functions'. These powers would enable the registrar to inspect the files and to enquire into how and why they were used. He would also be able to advise on the setting up of files, to investigate complaints by data subjects, to check that computer systems met certain minimum security criteria, and to refuse them registration if they did not. Any use of an unregistered system would be a crime, with anyone who suffered damage as a result able to take action in the civil courts. It would also be possible for complaints to be dealt with by the parliamentary ombudsman, by the health service, and by other bodies.

At that time (early-1981) the Government remained opposed to the idea of compulsory codes of practice for computer users. Voluntary codes, it has been suggested, could be devised by such groups as banks, airlines and market research bureaux for their own purposes. Police files would not be open to public scrutiny. Mr Raison noted that 'It would defeat the object of criminal intelligence records if suspects could get at the information they contain', and exceptions would also be made 'in the interests of protecting State security [and] the monetary interests of the State'.

By March 1982 it was clear that the Government was remaining firm in its commitment not to have a multimember data protection authority to supervise and enforce data protection legislation. At the European Information Technology and Management Exhibition at the Barbican in February, Mr Raison reasserted that the necessary functions would be undertaken by a single registrar who would be appointed by the Government – and who would be assisted by a staff of around twenty individuals.

The legislation is now promised for the next parliamentary session (writing in July 1982). It is thought that any computer system in which the name and address of individuals are recorded will be subject to the terms of the Act. The new law could even cover a word processing system which handles standard letters and stores details of to whom they are to be sent. Certain core principles will be based on those formulated by the 1972 Younger Committee (see Chapter 3). Many observers have suggested that there is great scope for individual interpretation of the Younger principles and that the associated standards for compliance will be necessarily loose. It can be difficult to reduce general principles into detailed working rules which information users can observe. The UK Government clearly does not favour the US approach (where detailed rules have been incorporated in the statute itself) or the approach recommended by Lindop and adopted by various European countries (that of establishing independent data protection authorities).

Some large multinational companies, under pressure from other countries in which they operate and where data protection laws already exist, have already set up their own codes of practice. It is clear that the UK Government plans will permit such companies to maintain their existing codes unchanged or with only small alterations. (Perhaps for this reason the representatives of mainly large businesses who attended the Barbican conference welcomed the minister's speech.) Life may be less simple for the smaller companies without the same resources to design and administer a data protection scheme.

THE WHITE PAPER (Cmnd 8539)

This publication, made available in April 1982, begins by recalling a statement (made on 19th March 1981) of the Home Secretary in which he declared the Government's intention to introduce legislation on data protection. Then, after brief background information (on Younger, Lindop and the European Convention), eight principles* are presented which the Government proposes should be embodied in the legislation:

(i) The information shall be obtained and processed fairly and lawfully;

(ii) It shall be held for a specified and legitimate purpose or purposes;

(iii) It shall not be used or disclosed in a way incompatible with those purposes;

(iv) It shall be adequate, relevant, and not excessive in relation to the specified purposes;

(v) It shall be accurate and, where necessary, kept up to date;

(vi) It shall be kept in name-linked form for no longer than is necessary for the specified purposes;

(vii) The data subject shall have access to information held about him and be entitled to its correction or erasure where the legal provisions safeguarding personal data have not yet been complied with;

(viii) Appropriate security measures must be taken against unauthorised access, alteration or dissemination, accidental loss and accidental or unauthorised destruction of data.

It is stated that sanctions provided by the legislation will be designed to ensure that, subject to any permitted exemptions, data users comply with the principles. The Government believes that codes of practice – which Lindop recommended should be drawn up by a Data Protection Authority and have the force of law – may have value for some professional bodies, trade associations and other organisations; but that such codes should not have the force of law. Moreover the Government believes that it would not be practicable, 'without imposing an unacceptable burden on

* following Articles 5, 7 and 8 of the Convention. Reference is made in the White Paper to the general principles set out in the Younger Report (see Chapter 3 of the present book), principles which were broadly endorsed by the Lindop Committee and embodied in the Convention.

resources, to cover the whole field of personal data systems with statutory codes of practice within any reasonable timescale' (the Lindop Report suggests that some fifty or more codes would apply the general principles to the range of situations in which personal information is processed by computer-based systems).

A central proposal is that all users of data systems which automatically process information relating to identifiable individuals should register. It is acknowledged that a public register would help to meet the objective that the existence and purpose of personal data banks should be publicly known. The data user would be required to provide necessary information – about himself, the information he uses, where it has come from and to whom it is disclosed, and the purposes for which it is used. It will also be necessary to register any changes in these details.

The Registrar, to be appointed by the Government, will be able to make enquiries, to inspect data files, and to order modifications to be made to a system. He will be able to refuse registration if it is deemed that the applicant's arrangements do not comply with the general principles, and he will also be empowered, if a case warrants it, to strike a data user off the register or to take legal proceedings against him. The Registrar will be able to offer advice to data users and data subjects, but will not have the resources to supervise the operation of data users in detail.

Apart from various specified exemptions, there will be obligations on central government, local authorities, the police, nationalised industries and other public sector bodies to register in the same way as other computer users. In considering exemptions it is noted that the European Convention prohibits the processing of data 'revealing racial origin, political opinions or religious or other beliefs, health or sexual life and criminal convictions' unless the law provides appropriate safeguards. It is also emphasised that the Convention allows derogation from the general principles in the interests of:

— protecting State security, public safety, the monetary interests of the State or the suppression of criminal offences;
— protecting the data subject or the rights and freedoms of others.

The Government proposes that the legislation should not apply to data that needs to be safeguarded for the purposes of national security. Other exemptions will include 'some data needed by the police and other law enforcement agencies for the prevention and detection of crime'. It is also likely that in the interest of protecting the data subject, 'medical records and . . . sensitive information recorded by social workers' would be exempt. In such cases the computer user will have to be registered but it may be appropriate to restrict access by the data subject. It is further suggested that the collection and use of data solely for statistical and research purposes do not threaten the privacy of data subjects, and that the collection of information for the purposes of public records and other archives is already governed by specific legislation.

The Government recognises that the registration process 'will take a considerable time, perhaps two years' and that users of particular categories of data 'may not be able, for financial or other reasons, to meet the full requirements of the legislation until some time after registration'. It is pointed out that the European Convention allows for phased implementation of data protection arrangements.

The White Paper includes the Council of Europe Convention for Data Protection (as Annex A) and the OECD Recommendations Concerning Guidelines Governing the Protection of Privacy and Transborder Flows of Personal Data (as Annex B). Thus, out of the twenty-four pages of the White Paper, fewer than six are devoted to the Government's legislative proposals on privacy and data protection.

REACTIONS TO THE WHITE PAPER

General

The overall reaction to the White Paper has so far been broadly unsympathetic. There is a general view, outside government, that the legislative proposals are insufficient to meet the data protection needs of Britain. It is worth recording the reactions from various sources.*

* The NCC reactions are given in Appendix 2.

Sir Norman Lindop

The Government's earlier idea that the Home Office should serve as its own watchdog was originally criticised by Sir Norman Lindop (amongst others). He noted that central and local government are by far the largest users of computerised information systems affecting almost every aspect of the citizen's life. In such circumstances Lindop argued that the Home Office was hardly impartial or disinterested in the field of personal information ('One has only to consider its special and direct responsibility for the Metropolitan police and its overall concern with police matters; its involvement with immigration control; drug abuse; prison and probation services and their records; and its concern with national security, to appreciate that the Home Office is necessarily deeply involved with some of the most sensitive areas of personal data collection and handling in the public sector'). It is likely that comments of this sort influenced the Government in its move from the idea of the Home Office as sole watchdog to the proposal of an independent Registrar.

In an address (reported in *Computer Weekly*, 6/5/82) to the fourth annual Grace Hopper Lecture at Thames Polytechnic, Sir Norman Lindop described the White Paper as 'the latest in a long list of government hesitations and prevarications' on the subject. He observed that the White Paper was 'very sketchy' and expressed concern about the potential number of exemptions from control allowed in the proposals. The public sector, he suggested, represented the main danger to privacy because of the massive amount of sensitive data held about individuals in manual and computer systems. He argued for effective codes of practice, and for measures to allow the police and the national security systems to fall within the ambit of the legislation.

Computer Industry Reactions

In April 1982, immediately after the publication of the White Paper, the Institute of Data Processing Management – which represents around 7000 of the professionals who run computers in government and business – were reported to be considering a protest campaign against the 'grossly inadequate' methods proposed by the Government to protect the citizen against the misuse of computerised personal information. Mr Ted Cluff, the Institute's secretary-general, said that the Home Office would have done better to have produced nothing rather than producing a White Paper which 'will satisfy nobody'. He also expressed doubts that the proposed Registrar would be truly independent, and suggested that it was absurd to expect an individual to bring a civil action to correct an abuse in this area.

The Computing Services Association (CSA) – representing software, bureau and consultancy companies – expressed agreement with the White Paper's general line. Dr Doug Eyeions, the CSA director-general, stated that the Association agreed with the Government's rejection of Lindop's proposed Data Protection Authority since there was a need for 'the minimum of bureaucracy'. At the same time the CSA was concerned at the delays and what it felt were many unanswered questions. Dr Eyeions also expressed amazement that the White Paper 'contained so little detail given the time it has taken to produce'. Also there was a need for the legislation to cover manual files as well as computerised systems.

The President of the British Computer Society (BCS), Mr Peter Hall, noted that the Society 'welcomes the Government's decision to introduce a law on data protection, which is needed by both the public and the computing profession'. Furthermore, 'we are pleased that they accept the principles formulated by the Younger Report of 1972'. However, it is pointed out also that the BCS supported the Lindop proposals for statutory codes of practice ('we question whether the voluntary codes referred to in the White Paper will be satisfactory and we believe that the full benefits of data processing and modern techniques of information technology will only become available if the Government provides a proper legal framework for their use').

An editorial in *Computer Weekly* (15/4/82) referred to the White Paper as 'the dampest squib that has been seen in many a season'. Further, the White Paper is 'a mass of vagueness that would make the Delphic oracle seem as explicit as an Algol program'. Specific objections relate to the number of exemptions from control ('there are bound to be claims that the legislation is pointless'), the arbitrary power of the Registrar, and the overall lack of precision in defining certain key proposals. It is concluded that legislation may be passed before important questions have been answered, and we would then be faced 'with the task of implementing woolly and dangerously flawed laws'. A later *Computer Weekly* (29/4/82) lists what are regarded as the main criticisms of the White Paper:

- exemption from registration of the security forces and their unhindered access to the registered data banks of both public and private organisations;
- lack of independence of the Registrar, who is to be appointed by the Crown. Concern is also expressed about the independence of the appeals tribunal;
- the absence in the White Paper of any legally enforceable codes of practice on the use and implementation of computerised information systems;
- the absence of any mention of manual systems in the proposed legislation;
- the reliance on civil rather than criminal remedies where misuse is proven;
- the possibility that the legislation will not meet the Council of Europe's Convention on Data Protection in either its content or the timescales for its implementation.

One observer (Connor, 22/4/82) notes that the White Paper has been variously condemned as a 'white mouse', a 'whitewash' and 'pathetic', and lists the main criticisms as:

- there is no multimember Data Protection Authority;
- there are no regular inspections;
- there are no codes of practice;
- manual systems are exempt;
- data banks of national security and criminal intelligence are exempt;
- it will still take up to two years for the legislation to come into force.

Such observations are typical of reactions to the White Paper in computer journals. Thus an article in *Computer Talk* (19/4/82) carries the headline 'Ten Years from Younger – And Still We're No Further On Down the Road to Protection'. Similarly an article in *Minicomputer News* (June 1982) begins with the observation that 'After three years of promising a White Paper on data protection of automated personal information the Conservative Government of Margaret Thatcher has finally produced one which has been received with scepticism and wide criticism from within the computer industry itself as well as from civil liberty and pressure groups'. And the article concludes by noting that the whole thrust of the data protection debate in the UK will be towards 'getting far more into any proposed legislation than the Government has indicated it will provide'.

BMA Reaction

The British Medical Association expressed concern about a number of aspects of the White Paper, even going so far as to suggest that doctors would refuse to cooperate with the police on such matters as case conferences on battered babies if police systems were exempt from privacy control. A BMA spokesman also declared that the exclusion of manual systems from control was not acceptable for medical records, and the need for effective codes has been emphasised ('We are quite adamant about what is needed to protect patients. The codes must be compulsory. The Registrar must be independent of Government'). Furthermore it is unacceptable that abuse of computerised data will not be a criminal offence: civil remedies are seen as inadequate. These objections to the White Paper are contained in a BMA press statement (7/4/82).

NCCL Reaction

Patricia Hewitt, general secretary of the National Council for Civil Liberties, observed that the White Paper 'omits every system that actually causes people privacy problems', and that the bulk of complaints received by the NCCL concerned manual systems which were not covered at all by the proposals. In the light of the widespread dissatisfaction with the White Paper, the NCCL resolved to set up a working party to draft its own rival proposed legislation with the aim of introducing a Private Member's Bill.

CBI Reaction

In response to the White Paper, the Confederation of British Industry declared that the cost of registering every computer system under the Government's proposals will be out of all proportion to the amount of personal privacy being protected. At the same time the CBI urged that the data protection authority should bring criminal actions against firms which abuse the privacy rules, and it should not be left to people to bring private lawsuits. A CBI spokesman suggested that without tough laws, UK legislation would not be in line with the Council of Europe proposals. (The CBI view on registration is backed by the CSA and IBM against the NCCL who feel that all systems should be registered.)

ICSA Reaction

The Institute of Chartered Secretaries and Administrators (ICSA) responded to the White Paper by setting out four basic rights which, it suggests, should be available to all data subjects. These rights, as set out in an ICSA memorandum (accompanying a News Release, 18/6/82), are:

— the right to be informed of any data elements which might be passed to third parties outside the business, in particular:

  (a) the circumstances in which they would be transmitted;

  (b) the identities of the receivers of the data elements;

  (c) the reasons for the disclosure of data;

  (d) the sources from which these data elements would be obtained;

— the right to receive a copy of the information concerning the data subject on each occasion when it is published or passed to a third party;

— the right to have erroneous 'external' data corrected or deleted;

— the right of access to relevant personal data items where the data subject has grounds for belief that he has been unfairly treated; and where his claims are proved, the right to redress, whether or not the injustice arose out of incorrect or out-of-date 'internal' data or from incorrect use of accurate 'internal' data.

It is suggested that these rights should be embodied in legislation or in statutory codes of practice, and that such measures should be combined with a Public Register of Systems. The ICSA clearly endorses parts of the White Paper (eg the proposals for a register) but thinks, in common with most other organisations offering comment, that the Government proposals do not go far enough (eg the need for statutory codes is urged, going beyond the terms of the White Paper).

THE GOVERNMENT RESPONSE

Mr Timothy Raison, the Home Office Minister concerned, speaking at a meeting of the Parliamentary Information Technology Committee (Pitcom), declared: 'We reject the Lindop view that there is a need for a multimember Data Protection Authority, made up of a chairman and part-time appointed members. We prefer an individual full-time Registrar appointed by the Crown and independent of government. Suggestions that the Registrar would lack effective power are misplaced. He will have real teeth'. It is now suggested that the Registrar's powers would be backed by criminal sanctions against offenders. Mr Raison has suggested that 'de-registration' would be tantamount to putting a user out of business.

Mr Raison has also claimed that a substantial amount of the information held by police, including much of what is on the Police National Computer, will have to be registered ('The police are with us in wanting all data possible to come within the scheme – consistent with fully maintaining the efficiency and effectiveness of police work. Exemptions in this area will be kept to a minimum'). It is emphasised that all public-sector data users will have to be registered – apart from the specified exemptions. Publicity will be given to how transfers of data are made, and the public will have access to information about them.

Speaking at a plenary session of the First National Conference on Computers in Personnel (23/6/82), Mr Raison considered the question of exemptions from registration on the part of the data user and exemptions from the right of access to data on the part of the data subject. He suggested that those who wanted statutory codes of practice 'have not thought the matter through', emphasising that 'almost every data user has a different requirement for accuracy, relevance, currency, retention, collection and dissemination of data'. It is pointed out that statutory codes cannot be produced for every one of these situations ('Their preparation and update would place intolerable strains on public sector resources. And the work would delay the introduction of legislation and therefore impact adversely our trading position').

Later parts of the speech focus on the declared exemptions. The police, for example, will not be wholly exempt, and much of the information held on the Police National Computer will be fully accessible by the Registrar and fully accessible by data subjects. However, certain information, eg criminal intelligence, would have to remain secret, as would certain information in the medical field ('it may not be in the interests of the patient to know all the information about him'). It is emphasised that the exemptions will not be extended 'just because users might be inconvenienced by releasing data'. The European Convention does not allow exemption, for instance, for employers who wish to limit access to personal data concerning assessments of employee performance.

Mr Raison also pointed out that special provision may also be required for some other categories of data. Consideration is being given to whether regulations containing specific safeguards should be introduced for data revealing, for example, details of race, religion, sexual activities, political and criminal convictions. It is likely that domestic computer users would be exempt (such users, for instance, may maintain files of their friends' names and addresses). Mr Raison emphasised that it would not be desirable to retreat from the principle of universal or near-universal registration, 'losing in the process the publicly visible list of the full scope of national use of personal data'. The aim should be to make the registration process sufficiently straightforward for even the small user not to be able to suggest that it is 'unduly burdensome'.

He concluded by stressing the need for 'an atmosphere in which there is the highest possible degree of confidence that the individual citizen's interests are not being put at risk by the spread of this new technology'. 'That,' declared Mr Raison, 'is the prime objective of our proposals, and we must not place it in jeopardy'.

SUMMARY

This chapter has outlined some of the post-Lindop pressures on the UK Government to move to enact data protection, and has indicated the Government's response (mainly as represented in the April 1982 White Paper). Over this period – late 1970s and early 1980s – pressure has grown from various sources, such as international trading companies, civil rights groups, and departments of government.

The Government's response has evolved over this period: there has been a growing willingness to recognise the need for legislation, and some changes have occurred in the official attitudes to how such legislation should be framed (for instance, the Government has moved from the idea of the Home Office as sole data protection watchdog to the proposal for an independent Registrar). Many of the critics of the White Paper are urging a stronger line from the Government. There are real fears that if the legislation is based solely on the terms of the White Paper then the law on data protection will be inadequate for various reasons. To some extent the Government has already shown some sensitivity to the criticisms: for example, in its seeming willingness to countenance an enlarged role for criminal sanctions in helping to enforce the legislation.

The post-Lindop scene in the UK has been characterised by a number of identifiable phases:

- the development of a range of pressures on the Government for a Green (discussion) or a White (intention to legislate) Paper signalling a commitment to statutory data protection;
- the publication of the White Paper in April 1982;
- the response and discussion that followed publication.

There is some uncertainty about how soon legislation will be enacted. The Government has indicated that delays will be kept to a minimum, but there could be difficulties. The weight of criticism and the complexity of the subject may have discouraged the

Government from early legislation. It may be felt that more discussion is needed. And even after enactment, it will be some time before the specified registrations are accomplished.

In these circumstances it is likely that the time to fully operating UK data protection legislation, of whatever quality, will be measured in years rather than months. It is important that in this interim period the pressures for effective legislation be maintained and the discussion continued.

5 The Future

INTRODUCTION

Future developments in privacy legislation and system security will be influenced by many factors. Some will be purely technical, relating to how efficiently vast amounts of personal information can be collected, stored and used. Here we may ask – how rapidly can stored data be accessed? how efficiently can data be transferred from one computer system to another? how effective are the system safeguards embodied, for instance, in programming?

Other factors are commercial, relating to the protection of important company information and the growing need for firms to operate across national boundaries. In a world economy where companies are fighting for their share of the market, we may expect the commercial pressures for data protection to grow. At the same time it will be necessary to avoid national legislation that unduly hampers legitimate business activities involving 'transborder' data flows.

Civil rights pressures will influence the scope of future privacy legislation in the UK and elsewhere – though there is debate as to how extensive this influence will be. Whatever the ethics of human rights issues, such matters may not be the most pressing concerns of government. In this connection it is significant that many observers – in, for instance, both the technical and general press – are able to focus on the civil rights aspects of data protection. Hence, as one example, Graham Bunting and Sean Hallahan have declared in *Computerworld UK,* 11/2/81: 'The reason why we need privacy legislation is that the rights of the individual should be respected and given protection in law. That is reason enough. Other arguments only serve to cloud the issue'.

Other pressures that are likely to influence legislation derive from the interests of our European trading partners and from possible US concern about the seeming inadequacy of European data protection in an insecure world. It will be difficult for the UK to resist effective privacy legislation in circumstances where Europe, the US, Australia, Japan and other developed countries are recognising the need for practical and far-reaching measures in this field.

THE INTERNATIONAL SCENE

In 1978, when the Lindop Report was published, it was known that various countries had already passed data protection legislation or were about to do so. Existing legislation was effective in:

- Sweden (1973 Data Act);
- USA (1974 Privacy Act);
- West Germany (1977 Federal Data Act, effective in 1978; 1970 Hesse Act);
- Canada (1977 Human Rights Act, effective in 1978);
- France (1978 Data Processing and Freedom Act);
- Norway (1978 Personal Data Registers Act);
- Denmark (1978 Acts on personal data in private sector and on electronic data in public sector).

At that time, effective legislation was anticipated in various other countries (eg Austria, Belgium and Luxembourg).

The provisions in the various national laws varied widely and continue to do so (we may expect the factors referred to in the early part of this chapter to exert pressure for a more standardised and unified approach in future legal amendments and new laws). By 1982 wide-ranging legislation had become effective in many countries, but differed in character from one nation to another.

Sweden, a pioneer in this field, has a licence system supported by a Data Protection Board and with attention given to transborder data flows. Provisions in Norway cover both manual and computer-stored information, requiring licences for all types of systems. Federal and State laws in West Germany and national legislation in France also cover both manual and computer systems, with a DPA in France empowered to authorise transborder data flows and to insist on other regulations. Laws in Luxembourg, Austria and Denmark only relate to personal information held in computer-based systems. In Spain and Portugal there are constitutional provisions granting all citizens the right to protection of privacy. The various measures in the US and Canada only apply to the public sector.

Early in 1981, seven countries (with the UK absent at that time) signed the Council of Europe Convention on Data Protection. Pressures were evident at that time, as before and since, for the UK Government to enact relevant legislation. (*The Times*, 1/12/80, instanced the case of British businessmen 'running into trouble' because of the absence of privacy laws and cited the case of a British firm losing a contract for the production of 80,000 health cards for Sweden. This case occurred as far back as August 1974, and there is little more recent evidence that British business is suffering serious loss of trade through the absence of data protection laws in the UK. Many business men are concerned, however, that this may become a real problem in the future.) There are now growing pressures for the European nations to ratify the Council of Europe Convention, and it is likely that this will happen in due course. It is worth highlighting some of the Articles in the Convention (already discussed in Chapter 3):

Article 1 — The purpose of the Convention is to secure respect for the rights and fundamental freedoms of individuals and especially the right to privacy with regard to the automatic processing of personal data;

Article 3 — It will apply to both the public and private sector but a country can supply a list to the Council of Europe of certain categories of automated personal data files it does not wish to apply the Convention to;

Article 5 — Personal data will be obtained and processed fairly and lawfully, stored for specified and legitimate purposes, not be excessive in relation to its purpose and not be kept for longer than required;

Article 6 — Personal data revealing religious or political opinions, criminal convictions and racial origins will not be stored 'unless domestic law provides appropriate safeguards';

Article 7 — Appropriate measures will be taken to prevent unauthorised access, alteration or dissemination;

Article 8 — Any person shall be able to establish the existence and main purposes of an automated personal data file and a copy of any personal data held about him or her. An individual should have the right to obtain a correction or erasure of any data processed contrary to the provisions of domestic law and have a remedy if such a request is not complied with;

Article 9 — Exceptions to Articles 5 to 8 should only be allowed in the interests of State security, public safety, the fiscal interests of the State, the suppression of criminal offences and to protect the data subject or the rights and freedoms of others. In addition parts of Article 8 may be suspended for scientific research purposes where there is obviously no risk of an infringement of the privacy of the data subjects;

Article 12 — Countries which have signed the Convention will not impede the flow of data between itself and other signatories.

In early-March 1982, Socialist members of the Strasbourg European Parliament failed to pass a directive aimed at bringing forward compulsory ratification of the Convention. Right-wing opponents of the directive claimed that it would be too expensive to implement, whereas those in favour of the directive emphasised the need to strengthen the legislation in order to meet the 'serious threat to the rights of the individual which data banks represent'. By mid-March a resolution had been passed calling on the EEC to issue a directive requiring member states to implement data protection measures before the end of 1982.

The resolution, going beyond UK Government proposals, demands that all data banks (public and private), containing information on private individuals, should be subject to authorisation and registration; that all individuals should be allowed to know what information is held about them and where; that individuals should be allowed to correct wrong or misleading entries; and that people should be entitled to damages resulting from the use of wrong information. The resolution also calls for the creation of an EEC regulatory body, in addition to whatever national measures are adopted.

A potential conflict has been pointed out between the requirements of the Convention and the demands of the European Parliament. The Convention excludes national security systems (eg MI5 and MI6) from regulation, whereas the resolution implies that all systems should be covered.

Whatever the requirements of Strasbourg or the Convention, individual member states continue to implement (or not) data protection measures according to how they evaluate their interests. The UK Government, for instance, is likely to be influenced by European pressures but will also take many other factors into account. One of these is sure to be how other countries have fared with their own legislation. It has been recognised, for example, that many French organisations are breaking the law with impunity by failing to register details of their data banks with the government. One estimate suggested (late-1981) that only 31,000 out of 150,000 bodies possessing computer-based files have obeyed orders to register with the State-sponsored CNIL (National Commission for Individual Rights and Freedom). It is noted that the average French citizen has personal information recorded in about 50 data banks operated by mail order houses, political organisations and other government and commercial users. However, not many people are aware that for a small fee (about 20 francs) they can request a written record of information about themselves which is held on the register.

It is obvious that the international data protection scene is very variable from one country to another, and also within some countries. The US, Australia and New Zealand, for example, have local state legislation as well as, in some cases, national laws. And different national considerations can affect attitudes to data protection. For instance, in the US, many companies regard privacy legislation as a new form of protectionism.

It is argued that the laws in some countries give competitors the right to look at heretofore confidential information, and that such a facility could give European companies an advantage, in terms of international trade, over US firms. Michael Blumenthal, chairman of Burroughs, suggested at the National Computer Conference that European data protection policies were harmful to trade. He observed that Burroughs expected to 'experience restriction on routine internal automations that depend on the free flow of information'. A number of other companies have also expressed concern. A T & T recently produced a 52-page report for executives, outlining threats to international data flows; and IBM, American Express and Chase Manhattan Bank have all created study groups to examine what they see as the difficulties posed by foreign data protection policies. Measures are being proposed to enable US companies to take concerted action to protect their interests.

Elsewhere, countries are continuing to develop national and local data protection provisions. Japan, for example, is expected to introduce a comprehensive data protection policy in the spring. The Japanese government has acknowledged the public concern over increasing threats to personal privacy, and is committed to implementing guidelines on privacy protection and international transfer of personal data, as drawn up by the Organisation for Economic Co-operation and Development (OECD). More than half those interviewed in a recent Japanese survey believed that privacy violations were becoming more numerous in their computerised society.

SYSTEM DESIGN FOR SECURITY

Security has always been a consideration in good systems design. It is now clear that new data protection provisions are likely to affect traditional systems analysis and design procedures. Since many end users may not be expected to know the details of forthcoming legislation bearing on computers, the responsibility for ensuring that systems meet new regulations is likely to fall on the analyst. A systems development manager has been quoted in *Datalink* (1/3/82): 'I doubt that anyone pushing through the legislation has done their sums on the sheer number of systems that will have to be approved. Either the registration is going to be a mere rubber stamp formality or it's going to be chaos'. It is suggested that many programmers and analysts may see data protection legislation as an irritating inconvenience, though as concerned as anyone else about the issues at stake.

Systems designers will be obliged to see registration as part of the system implementation process. The user will be required to inform the Registrar about the contents of his data bank, but it is the analyst who will have advised him how to secure the information. The task of the analyst, in having to take into account an unprecedented level of security, will be more complicated than hitherto. This circumstance may be expected to increase the costs of systems analysis and design, a development that is unlikely to be welcomed by many companies in a difficult trading position.

The growing need for security, with or without new legislation, is already being reflected in many system designs. Tutt (1982), for example, describes the Bankers' Automated Clearing Services (Bacs) facility as 'one of the most protected, secure and even molly-coddled computer installations in the country'. Increasingly, under the pressure of new regulations, security will be seen as a prime requirement in system design.

AUDITING FOR PRIVACY

The possibility of auditing for privacy, in the light of likely data protection legislation, is being considered by various organisations. The Department of Industry funded half of a £70,000 project aimed at investigating the idea of providing a data privacy audit for companies at the same time as a financial audit. The rest of the money for the experiment, involving six organisations, was provided by The National Computing Centre and Deloitte Haskins & Sells. NCC Director, David Fairbairn, has declared: 'We wanted to see if you could carry out an accurate privacy audit at the same time as a financial one and how much additional work it would involve. The preliminary results are very promising'. It has been estimated that the scheme would be of particular interest to the top 500-1000 companies in the UK, all of which maintain computer-based files of information.

The results of the investigation are contained in the recent NCC report, *The External Auditor as Privacy Inspector**. Ian Douglas, a

* More details are given of this report in Appendix 3

senior consultant at NCC, has observed that the audit could be used by the Registrar heralded in the Government's legislative proposals (Douglas: 'It seems pointless having a Registrar if he doesn't have a watchdog. Computer audits could be that watchdog, if the auditors were certified by the Registrar'). However, he has also pointed out that it is impractical to validate the information on file – 'all you can say is that a company is taking reasonable steps to protect it'. Furthermore, there is always the possibility that a tape kept in a safe has been copied. Further public discussion of the privacy audit possibility is anticipated.

SUMMARY

The UK and international data protection scene is developing rapidly. There are national and international pressures for a unification of existing regulations and for new legislation where existing measures are deemed to be inadequate. There is considerable variation from one country to another in prevailing and intended data protection legislation.

Data protection provisions have consequences for system design and operation. Security concepts need to be given proper attention, placing responsibility with analysts and designers. Once systems intended to hold personal data have been designed and implemented, it will be necessary – under the UK Government's intended legislation – to register details of such systems (and other defined classes of information) with the Crown-appointed Registrar. Privacy audits, conducted in independent organisations, have been represented as a means whereby the systems in question can be shown to satisfy the relevant conditions specified in the legislation.

There is a broad consensus in the UK on the need for effective legislation on data protection, though there is much debate about the form such legislation should take. It is important that discussion continue – with the objective of effective legislation that safeguards the individual citizen and social groups without impeding the legitimate activities of companies, government departments and other organisations. As with much legislation, there is a balance to be struck, but this should be attempted with the clear acknowledgement that there are vital human rights issues at stake. Privacy legislation should be more than a costly and bureaucratic accretion in the world of technology: it concerns the quality of life in democratic society.

APPENDIX 1

Bibliography

CHAPTER 1

Elbra T, Talking Security, *NCC Interface*, January 1982, p 7

Jones M, *Privacy,* David & Charles, 1974

Harrington T, A DP Project to Put Fear in a Tax Evader's Heart, *Computing*, 8/9/82, pp 30-31

Kling R, Social Analyses of Computing, *Information Age*, January 1982, pp 25-55

Lamb J, Are Forbidden Files as Secure as They Ought to Be? *Computer Talk*, 29/3/82

Lansdown J, Ethics of Computer Use, *Information Privacy*, September 1981, pp 178-179

Lobel J, Public Good Versus Public Harm Potential of Computers, *Information Age*, April 1982, pp 75-78

Madgwick D and Smythe T, *The Invasion of Privacy*, Pitman, 1974

Parker D, Future of Computer Security, *Information Age*, January 1982, pp 15-18

Pritchard J, Why You Should Take Another Look at Encryption, *Data Processing*, October 1980, pp 15-17

Privacy, Computers and You, NCC Publications, 1972

Rule J, *Private Lives and Public Surveillance: Social Control in the Computer Age*, Schocken, USA, 1974

Sharpe R, Data Flow: the US Takes on Europe, *Computing*, 28/5/81, pp 16-17

Westin A and Baker M, *Databanks in a Free Society: Computers, Record-keeping and Privacy*, Quadrangle, USA, 1972

Yang T L, Privacy in English and American Law, *International and Comparative Law Quarterly*, January 1966

CHAPTER 2

BMA Privacy Push Picks Up Speed, *Computer Talk*, 14/9/81

Breaking Silence on the Data Held by MI5, *Computing*, 4/3/82, p 13

Burton R P, Transnational Data Flows: International Status, Impact and Accommodation, *Data Management*, June 1980, pp 27-33

Connor S, Police Move in to Hit the 'Grey Areas' of Civilian Control, *Computing*, 9/7/81, p 21

Connor S, The Police Intelligence Database is Put on Trial, *Computing*, 18/2/82, pp 24-25

Connor S, Commons Snubbed by MI5, *Computing*, 11/3/82, p 14

Connor S, How Your Records Start Growing Up from Birth, *Computing*, 22/4/82, pp 22-23

Gassman H P, Privacy Implications of Transborder Data Flows: Outlook for the 1980s, *Computers and Privacy in the Next Decade*, Academic Press, 1980

Gelinas U, Transborder Dataflows: Key Issues and an Implementation Mechanism, *Information Privacy*, July 1981, pp 131-136

Hattersley Takes Up MI5 Secrecy Debate, *Computing*, 8/4/82, p 11

Johnston R, Doctors Threaten Boycott Over Data Protection, *Computer Weekly*, 24/9/81, p 3

Jones M, *Privacy*, David & Charles, 1974

Kennett D and Pearson K, MP Slams Lack of Control Over Police Systems, *Computer Weekly*, 25/3/82, p 2

Kling R, Computer Abuse and Computer Crime as Organisational Activities, *Information Privacy*, September 1981, pp 186-195

Lamb J, Are Forbidden Files as Secure as They Ought to Be? *Computer Talk*, 29/3/82

Leigh D, Alderson Scraps Files of Special Branch, *Observer*, 10/1/82

Leigh D, Special Branch's Dossier on SDP Member Revealed, *Observer*, 31/1/82

Lundin J, Police Act to Stop Computer Leaks, *Observer*, 8/11/81

Madgwick D and Smythe T, *The Invasion of Privacy*, Pitman, 1974

McLauchlan W, Privacy and Criminal Justice, *Information Privacy*, March 1981, pp 43-49

MPs Attack MI5 Secret Installation, *Computing*, 11/3/82

MP Seeks Police Computer Probe, *Computing*, 18/2/82

Norton-Taylor R, Policeman Suspended Over Computer 'Leaks', *Guardian*, 24/10/81

Pallister D, Softly, Softly Approach to New Police Data Link, *Guardian*, 22/3/82

Parry G, Police Computer 'Needs MP Watchdogs', *Guardian*, 22/3/82

Pithers M, Computer Plan is Denied to Yorkshire Police, *Guardian*, 22/1/82

Police Buy £1.5m Fingerprint System, *Computing*, 3/6/82

Pounder C, Vehicle Checks Increase, *Computing*, 11/3/82, pp 28-29

Pounder C and Anderson S, *The Police Use of Computers*, Technical Authors Group (Scotland), Occasional Publication No. 1, 1982

Private Lives and Public Computers, *New Scientist*, 28/1/82, p 216

Turn R, Transborder Dataflows: Privacy Protection, *Information Privacy*, March 1981, pp 56-67

Turn R, Transborder Dataflows: Implementation of Privacy Protection, *Information Privacy*, May 1981, pp 98-119

Veitch A, Computer Data Leak Report Starts Inquiry, *Guardian*, 8/8/81

Veitch A, Computerisation Plans for Medical Records Gather Pace, *Guardian*, 19/10/81

Watchdog's Silence Proves Owner's Guilt, *Computing*, 1/4/82, p 13

Westin A, Privacy Issues in Personnel Administration, *Information Age*, January 1982, pp 5-14

Westin A, Computer Use in Personnel Administration, *Information Age*, April 1982, pp 95-114

Whitelaw Discloses Bugging Code, *Guardian*, 26/2/82

CHAPTER 3

Committee of Ministers, *Council of Europe Convention for the Protection of Individuals with regard to Automatic Processing of Personal Data*, Strasbourg, France, 18/9/80

Computers and Privacy, Cmnd 6353, HMSO, 1975

Computers: Safeguards for Privacy, Cmnd 6354, HMSO, 1975

Connor S, Lindop Takes Privacy Out into the Open, *Computing*, 22/10/81, pp 30-31

Council of Ministers, Organisation for Economic Co-operation and Development, *OECD Guidelines Governing the Protection of Privacy and Transborder Flows of Personal Data*, 523rd Meeting, 23/9/80

Data Protection, The Government's Proposals for Legislation, Cmnd 8539, HMSO, April 1982

Jones M, *Privacy*, David & Charles, 1974

Madgwick D and Smythe T, *The Invasion of Privacy*, Pitman, 1974

Miller A R, *Assault on Privacy: Computers, Data Banks and Dossiers*, University of Michigan Press, 1971

Pitcher H H W, NCC Codes of Practice for Data Protection, *Information Privacy*, July 1981, pp 137-164

Report of the Committee on Data Protection (Sir Norman Lindop, Chairman), Cmnd 7341, HMSO, 1978

Report of the Committee on Privacy (The Rt Hon Kenneth Younger, Chairman), Cmnd 5012, HMSO, 1972

Samet P, Younger, Lindop and the Microprocessor, *Information Age*, April 1982, pp 67-68

Sauverin P T, Privacy – the Commonsense Application of Authority, *Information Privacy*, November 1979, pp 322-325

Sauverin P T, User Preparation for Compliance with Forthcoming UK Data-Protection Legislation, *Information Age*, April 1982, pp 69-74

CHAPTER 4

A Damp Squib on Data Protection, *Computer Weekly*, 15/4/82

BMA Still Concerned Over Details of Patients' Records in Data Protection White Paper, BMA Press Statement, London, 7/4/82

Brown C, PM Promises Tighter Controls of Data Banks, *Guardian*, 10/2/82

Connor S, Lindop Takes Privacy Out Into the Open, *Computing*, 22/10/81, pp 30-31

Connor S, Critics Give Protection White Paper a Pasting, *Computing*, 22/4/82, p 18

Data Protection Legislation: The Justification for Exemptions, Home Office News Release, 23/6/82

Data Protection — The Government's Proposals for Legislation, Cmnd 8539, HMSO, April 1982

Eleven Years of Urgent Action, *Guardian*, 10/2/82

Government Admits Privacy Defeat, *Computer Talk*, 22/2/82

Important Role for Users in Government Data Legislation Plans, *Computer Management*, September 1981

Johnston R, Government Puts Off Privacy Law Again, *Computer Weekly*, 12/11/81

Johnston R, Government Favours Independent Privacy Control, *Computer Weekly*, 18/2/82, p 3

Johnston R, Revolt on Government Plans for Data Protection, *Computer Weekly*, 15/4/82, p 1

Large P, Britain to Sign on Computer Privacy, *Guardian*, 8/5/81

Large P and Norton-Taylor R, Computer Protection Law Faces Delay Until 1985, *Guardian*, 8/4/82, p 28

Large P, Attack on Data Privacy Proposals, *Guardian*, 10/4/82

Mikardo to Push Government on Privacy Issue, *Computerworld UK*, 11/2/81, p 5

Park M, Analysts Face New Security Headache, *Datalink*, 1/3/82, p 7

Park M, Abuse of Data is Criminal Says the BCS, *Datalink*, 26/4/82, p 3

Pearson K, Lindop Joins Outcry on Privacy White Paper, *Computer Weekly*, 6/5/82

Privacy of Data Subjects Must be Protected, Institute of Chartered Secretaries and Administrators (ICSA) News Release, 18/6/82

Privacy Watchdog to Bite, *Computer Talk*, 10/5/82

Raison Wrong on Data Privacy, *Electronics Weekly*, 24/6/81, p 4

Riley T, Data Privacy White Paper, *Minicomputer News*, June 1982, pp 10-11

Sedacca B, 'Data Abuse Will Mean Criminal Sanctions' Says Minister, *Computer Weekly*, 13/5/82, p 2

Ten Years From Younger — And Still We're No Further on Down the Road to Protection, *Computer Talk*, 19/4/82

UK Privacy Law Due in New Year, *Computing*, 24/9/81

Veitch A, Data Protection Plan Under Fire from All Sides, *Guardian*, 16/9/81

Veitch A, Home Office May Accept Watchdog for Files, *Guardian*, 19/1/82

Whitelaw Faces New Privacy Quiz, *Computer Talk*, 15/2/82, p 1

Wright J, Safeguarding the Individual, *Computing*, 4/3/82, p 28

CHAPTER 5

Bunting G and Hallahan S, Wrong Case for Privacy Legislation, *Computerworld UK*, 11/2/81, p 3

Coffey M, US Takes a Dim View of European Data Laws, *Computing*, 8/10/81

Connor S, Sussex Solves Problems of Student Information, *Computing*, 17/6/82, p 23

Council of Europe Convention, *Information Privacy*, July 1981, pp 165-171

Deloitte Haskins & Sells and The National Computing Centre, *The External Auditor as Privacy Inspector*, NCC, 1982

DOI Funds Privacy Audit Experiment, *Computing*, 25/3/82, p 9

Donker M, France Journeys Into the Privacy Minefield, *Computing*, 4/2/82

Gee J, Computer File Organisations 'Breaking Law', *Computer Weekly*, 8/10/81

Gelinas U, Transborder Dataflows: Key Issues and an Implementation Mechanism, *Information Privacy*, July 1981, pp 131-136

Hallahan S and May M, The Business of Privacy, *Computerworld UK*, 11/2/81, pp 20-21

Huggins T, 'Privacy Audit' Is Proposed by NCC, *Computing*, 24/6/82, p 8

OECD Recommendations on Transborder Flows, *Information Privacy*, September 1981, pp 203-216

Park M, Analysts Face New Security Headache, *Datalink*, 1/3/82, p 7

Pearson K, EEC Calls for Wider Law on Data Privacy, *Computer Weekly*, 18/3/82, p 1

Tutt N, Guarding Bacs with Checks and Balances, *Computing*, 17/6/82, p 25

Walton P, EEC Vetoes Boost to Data Protection, *Computing*, 18/3/82

Westin A F, Home Information Systems: The Privacy Debate, *Datamation*, July 1982, pp 100, 103-104, 106, 111-112, 114

APPENDIX 2

NCC Response to White Paper (Cmnd 8539)

Michael Wood and Tony Elbra

NCC RESPONSE TO WHITE PAPER (Cmnd 8539)

Extract from letter (26/5/82) from Michael Wood (Manager, Privacy and Security Division) to the Home Office:

'The National Computing Centre welcomes the publication of firm proposals for action in this important area.

We are disappointed that codes of practice have not found favour as a mechanism for legal regulation of data use. Our own work on codes of practice supported by the Department of Industry, showed that this mechanism was both effective so far as the interest of the data subject is concerned, and acceptable to data users. A relatively small number of codes – perhaps 10 or 20 – would cover almost all commercial applications, except for those relatively very few systems handling particularly sensitive data. For such systems the Registrar, perhaps with the help of the proposed Advisory Committee, could devise appropriate codes to give the necessary additional safeguards for the interests of the data subject.

The White Paper does not provide adequate guidance for those who are implementing systems at the present time. We urge that this guidance should be provided at the earliest possible time. Many systems today are intended to last for ten years, and changes are costly and difficult to implement after installation.

We have commented in detail on the individual paragraphs of the White Paper where we felt it appropriate to do so . . .'.

DETAILED COMMENTS ON WHITE PAPER (Cmnd 8539) (Michael Wood and Tony Elbra)

Appropriate paragraph details from the White Paper ('Data Protection: the Government's Proposals for Legislation') are given with the associated NCC comments. Readers wanting the full text should refer to the White Paper.

Paragraph 6 refers to the 'general principles set out in the Younger Report' and claims to list them, 'following Articles 5, 7 and 8' of the Council of Europe Convention. *Paragraph 7* proposes 'that these principles should be embodied in the legislation'. However, some of these principles or parts of them are ignored in the White Paper.

Principle no. 1 stated that information 'should be held for a specific purpose and not be used, without appropriate authorisation, for other purposes'.

The option to extend the purpose through authorisation has been omitted in these proposals.

Principle no. 6 stated that 'the level of security should be specified in advance by the user . . .'.

Principle no. 7 stated that 'a monitoring system should be provided to facilitate the detection of any violation of the security system'.

Any legally required monitoring system must be limited to recording accesses and detecting unauthorised attempts to access. It will not be possible to prove that no unauthorised access has taken place in the past, but the system must ensure that any attempt is made as difficult as possible.

Principle no. 8 stated that 'periods should be specified beyond which the information should not be retained'.

Principle no. 10 stated that 'care should be taken in coding value judgements'.

Principle no. 4 (statistical systems) is dealt with later under para. 15.

Principles nos. 6, 7, 8 and 10 are ignored in these proposals.

We are not sorry to see Principle no. 8 dropped, as it offers possible conflict with archiving and research interests. We also regard its strict legal enforcement as placing an unnecessary burden on computer users, who would be required to ensure that every copy on magnetic media and on paper were destroyed after the stated time. It seems better to allow the normal commercial pressures to save space and computer equipment to dictate the erasure of out-of-date files.

(On Principle no. 6 see the comments below on Para. 9.)

Value judgements, which are based on opinion rather than fact, must obviously be used with care. Any code used should be decoded on the copy of the record made available to the data subject.

Point no. (viii) goes beyond the Younger Principles in requiring that security measures be taken against accidental loss or destruction of data. This is in accordance with Article 7 of the Council of Europe Convention. This additional requirement should be removed. The loss or destruction of data is in itself a blow to the data user, which should not be made worse by the imposition of legal sanctions.

Paragraph 7 states that the term 'data user' includes those who collect data, collate or otherwise process data by automatic means, and disseminate data.

The term 'data user' as defined leaves unanswered a good many questions. For example, a collector of data using manual techniques for subsequent automatic processing may or may not be covered by this definition. Similarly, a disseminator of printed data previously processed has an uncertain classification.

Data can move rapidly between paper form, microfilm and magnetic media, and it seems ridiculous to apply the law only to computer data, ignoring paper and leaving microfilm somewhere between the two. At least the restrictions on access should apply to all forms or representations of the data that is protected.

The Government proposals say nothing about word processing and free-text systems. The suggested law would give rise to anomalies in this area as for example, published material could exist legally in book form and become subject to the legislation as soon as it was entered on a text processor.

Paragraph 8 refers to the codes of practice recommended by the Lindop Committee — 'The Government does not consider that these codes should have the force of law or that it would be practicable, without imposing an unacceptable burden on resources, to cover the whole field of personal data systems with statutory codes of practice within any reasonable timescale. The Government accepts, however, that in some areas . . . the general principles will need to be supplemented by regulations'.

The law should be as simple as possible and should not require a number of sub-sections only applicable to one particular application. The use of Codes of Practice allows the law to state the basic principles required; while the interpretation of them in each circumstance is spelt out in the appropriate Code of Practice. In this way, the simplicity of the law is maintained while each data user is required to understand only those parts of the Codes of Practice that directly concern him.

The degree of control necessary must depend on the nature of the data to be handled. It is undesirable to place unnecessary constraints on the less sensitive areas only because they are required in the more sensitive ones. A series of Codes of Practice would enable the degree of control to be adjusted to the requirements of the application.

The Registrar will be required to examine each application as it is presented to him and determine if it is acceptable in the light of the principles of data protection. For his own use he will need to draw up some criteria that can be applied in like cases. We suggest that these criteria be published. Then they will form a known Code of Practice which will be available to systems designers, enabling them to know if a system is acceptable before they submit it.

It is envisaged that the Codes of Practice be developed by the Registrar as the need arises, using such professional advice as is necessary. They would not form part of the law, but would indicate the way in which the law is to be interpreted.

Paragraph 9 indicates the necessary requirements in setting up a public register.

While agreeing that requirements for registration should be as simple as possible, it is important that they should also be meaningful. For each application, the user should state the type of subject that it covers (eg customer, employee) and the sort of information that is held (eg name, address, credit rating). The level of security relevant to each application should also be stated in accordance with Younger Principle no. 6.

Paragraph 11 outlines the anticipated resources of the Registrar.

The staff of twenty which is envisaged may well be too small to give a reasonable service; this is particularly likely during the initial rush. To help in this, it is recommended that data users be given a sufficiently long period in which to comply with the legislation. It is important that the Registrar is not seen only as an obstruction to the successful implementation of computer systems; to that end his staff should be large enough and the requirements of registration should be simple enough to guarantee a speedy service.

The Registrar should have the power to investigate complaints by members of the public and to hold hearings (see Lindop 38, 29-33). The result of his investigations may be an order to correct or delete certain data and/or the imposition of a fine. He should not, however, have the power to award damages. Any decision by the Registrar will be subject to appeal to the Appeal Tribunal.

All this may be the Government's intentions but those are not made clear in this document.

Paragraph 14 declares that the 'power to make regulations . . . will be needed to deal with, amongst other things, the processing of categories of data where it is not sufficient to rely on the general principles alone and where Parliament may expect to see detailed requirements laid down'.

Article 6 of the Convention of the Council of Europe prohibits the automatic processing of certain categories of data unless the law provides safeguards. Since our present law does not, it follows that such data may not be processed. The White Paper mentions the need to make regulations, but without giving any idea what such regulations could be. It seems logical to introduce these regulations at the same time as the law regarding data privacy, since until the special categories of data are covered, we cannot be said to comply with the Convention.

Plainly it is not practical to prohibit the use of such data effectively. For example, churches and political parties may wish to keep computerised membership lists.

Paragraph 15 states that the 'collection and use of the data solely for statistical or research purposes does not threaten the privacy of data subjects, provided that in processing and disseminating the results steps are taken against revealing information about an identifiable individual'.

Data held for statistical or research purposes is innocuous only if an individual's data cannot be readily identified. For this reason, data held for these purposes should be exempt only if it is no longer in name linked form.

If this condition is met, then data collected for one purpose can be transferred to statistical or research files without the consent of the subject.

Paragraph 16 states that the 'collection of information for the purposes of public records and other archives is already governed by specific legislation' and that it is not intended 'that the data protection legislation should inhibit the preservation of historically valuable data for these purposes'.

This paragraph requires some explanation. It is impossible to say what information will interest the historian and today's trivia may be seen tomorrow as very significant. This being so, it appears that this clause will allow a wide area of non-compliance with the rest of the legislation.

Paragraph 17 refers to exemptions from the legislation (such categories as systems relating to State security, public safety, the monetary interests of the State, and the suppression of criminal offences).

It should be remembered that the intended legislation deals only with personal data, so subjects such as military dispositions, state finances, etc, are excluded from the start.

In some of these categories at least it would be unwise to let the data subject see his record. But, given this restriction, there seems to be no reason why all the other aspects of the proposed legislation should not apply to those records. Lindop specifically excluded some police files from any special treatment (Lindop 38, 51) but suggested that data relevant to national security, etc, be placed on a special register (Lindop 38, 20).

We suggest that registration of and enquiry into the special categories of data covered by this paragraph be undertaken by a member of the Registrar's staff who has been given the necessary security clearance.

Paragraph 18 declares that 'those who use computer bureaux will have to register, as will the bureaux themselves'.

Whereas the data user may expect to control the purpose, collection, dissemination of and access to the data, the bureau will usually be able to influence many of these functions. The bureau's activities may be carried out rightly or erroneously or indeed with criminal intent, and it would be invidious to place all the burden of compliance on the data user.

Paragraph 19 discusses the approach to sanctions. We would suppose that any sanctions imposed by the Registrar will be subject to appeal.

Paragraph 20 deals with the availability of civil remedies for data subjects who have suffered damage. The subject has the right to claim for damages through the courts. It would appear that the clearest way to establish liability on behalf of the data user would be through a previous adverse decision by the Registrar. Similarly, the data user could establish his freedom from liability by a decision in his favour.

Although data should be accurate, complete and up-to-date, these requirements should be considered in the light of the needs of the system under consideration. For example, a system that is run monthly only requires monthly updates. Complete accuracy can never be guaranteed and it should be sufficient for the data user to show that he had taken all reasonable steps to ensure that the data was accurate, having regard to its significance and sensitivity.

Paragraph 22, stating that the Government will be able to restrict the transfer of categories of information to specified countries whose laws do not provide comparable safeguards . . . suggests that the Government may restrict the flow of data abroad, but does not say how this will be done. A possible control would be the requirement to license the export of data in advance. A complication is that, even with countries having data protection legislation, different views persist as to what is private. Some countries prohibit the dissemination of addresses, while permitting the publication of income tax figures.

Paragraph 24 states that a data subject will be expected to pay a fee in order to gain access to information about him. In fact, an access fee is a common feature of most legislation, but is rarely charged. A better disincentive to frivolous access requests would be a limit on the number that may be made (say, one a year). But in the event of incorrect data being found, the data subject should have the right to expect that all other organisations that have had access to that data over a reasonable period, should be informed of the correction.

Paragraph 26 notes that the Convention allows for a phased implementation of data protection arrangements.

We welcome the proposal for a phased implementation of the legislation giving data users a chance to prepare properly for it.

In particular we hope that:

(i) the legal restrictions on access will apply to departments and sections of the organisation rather than individuals;

(ii) the legislation will allow such free flow of information as is normally enjoyed, eg communication between departments of the same organisation; output of credit and debit records to the Bankers Automated Clearing Services; collection of union dues, voluntary contributions, etc.

If the legislation is made unnecessarily rigorous in this respect, it will make its implementation by data users harder, and this may delay compliance with the law.

In general we would welcome clarification of the following:

Legal Persons. Will the legislation cover legal persons as well as natural persons? We believe that it should not, but sensitive personal data traceable to individuals should be covered wherever it appears.

Source and Destination of Data. Should the data user be required to reveal the source and destination of any data that is found to be incorrect? We believe that he should not, as the data user must be expected to respect the confidence of those that supply him with data and those that use his output. However, the data user must inform both the source and users of his data of any correction that is required.

APPENDIX 3

Privacy Audit Investigation

Deloitte Haskins & Sells and The National Computing Centre agreed to co-operate in a joint study to assess the feasibility and effectiveness of using external auditors to inspect the privacy aspects of commercial and industrial systems. A proposal to this effect was made to the Computers, Systems and Electronics Requirements Board in November 1980 and support was requested for half the total project costs. The project was approved, and the procedure and findings were subsequently published in July 1982 as a 51-page report, *The External Auditor as Privacy Inspector*.

The primary objective was to assess the feasibility of using external auditors to carry out privacy audits. Secondary objectives were:

— to determine the factors affecting the costing of a privacy inspection;

— to demonstrate any effects on the existing auditor/client relationship;

— to assess, as far as possible, the level of confidence which data subjects would have in the effectiveness of the inspection.

Section 4 of the report deals with the 'requirements of an effective privacy inspection'. It is emphasised that public confidence in the privacy of personal data can only be ensured if the privacy principles established by legislation are manifestly seen to have been effective. Drawing on the sets of privacy principles proposed in the Younger Report, the Lindop Report, the European Convention and in the OECD Guidelines, thirteen basic principles were listed as a basis for drawing up a set of criteria for privacy inspections. To ensure compliance with the privacy principles, the inspector:

— would carry out a review of the system, both manual and computer, and of the environment in which computer systems are developed, maintained and operated;

— would obtain an understanding of the system and procedures and identify the controls operated both manually and by computer program.

The inspector would identify the controls over: the completeness, accuracy and authorisation of input; the completeness and accuracy of processing; the maintenance of data held on file; and access to data held on file. It would be necessary to identify controls designed:

— to prevent or detect unauthorised changes to programs;

— to ensure that all program changes are adequately tested and documented;

— to prevent or detect errors during program execution;

— to prevent unauthorised amendments to data files;

— to ensure that systems software is properly installed and maintained;

— to ensure that proper documentation is kept;

— to ensure that access to files of data and output is physically restricted..

The inspector would then test the controls. Checks, using independent programs, may be placed on the data to establish its existence, accuracy, age and extent. It is recognised that to perform these tasks effectively the inspector should have appropriate training and skills, should be trustworthy, should understand organisational behaviour, should have an up-to-date knowledge of computer technology, and should understand the principles of data protection. (A table correlates the privacy principles to be inspected and the personal qualities required by inspectors.) When the checks are complete, the inspector could produce two types of report:

— the report on the data user's compliance with legislation, a report 'which we suggest should be required by law and filed with the Registrar';

— the confidential report to the organisation to draw attention to shortcomings and to suggest improvements.

The practical investigation which yielded *The External Auditor as Privacy Inspector* was managed jointly by a Partner of Deloitte Haskins & Sells and the Manager of the NCC Data Processing

Division. Teams were created to inspect computer-based systems holding personal data in six co-operating organisations:

— a computer centre operating a banking system for a number of banks (privacy controls);

— a bank using the computer centre (account-holder information);

— a life insurance company (policy-holder information);

— a manufacturing company (payroll);

— a university (student records);

— a local authority ('owner-occupier' ratepayer information).

It is emphasised that the 'data controller' should have sufficient authority to carry out his task effectively. None of the organisations investigated had appointed a data controller with specific responsibility to give effect to privacy principles. Some organisations suggested that the role of data controller could be performed by the head of the internal audit unit.

In Section 6 of the study, findings are reported in connection with the specific purpose of data use, the notification of data, special categories of data, whether minimum data was held, accuracy, the time limitation for retaining data, value judgements, statistics, access to data, security provisions and security monitoring.

Specific project findings are given (in Section 7) in relation to the external auditors' capabilities for privacy inspection, effects on the auditor/client relationship and costs. In checking the degree of compliance by organisations with the privacy principles, 'accuracy' and 'access' emerged as potential problem areas. These are seen as two principles which 'could present problems for the data user and the privacy inspector'.

Section 8 emphasises the need for the public at large, and the data subject in particular, to have confidence that only accurate personal data is held on file and that it is used only for authorised purposes. A process of 'certification' for inspectors of personal data is proposed, similar to the 'Practising Certificate' of Chartered and Certified Accountants.

Section 9 records that 'The consensus of client opinion was that a privacy inspection would be a natural and logical extension of an existing financial audit'.

Specific conclusions (given in Section 10) relate to the auditors' capabilities (external auditors, given a knowledge of auditing computer-based systems and an understanding of the principles of data protection, 'were well qualified to carry out data protection inspections'), the effects on the auditor/client relationship (no evidence that privacy inspections 'would in any way affect the existing good auditor/client relationship'), costs (materially less if privacy inspections were 'carried out as an extension of a financial audit'), and confidence (this 'would best be engendered by the certification of privacy inspectors').

Appendices profile privacy developments in the UK and elsewhere (Appendix A) and the current approach to financial auditing which has been accepted by the major professional accounting bodies (Appendix B).

APPENDIX 4

Index

Index